# Executive Compensation Answer Book

V.P. Kuraitis
Janet Ambrosi Wertman, Esq.

**THE PANEL ANSWER BOOK SERIES**

Copyright © 1992

by
PANEL PUBLISHERS, INC.
*A Wolters Kluwer Company*

36 West 44th Street
New York, NY 10036
(212) 790-2090

ISBN 1-878375-55-5

Printed in the United States of America

# About Panel Publishers, Inc.

Panel Publishers derives its name from a panel of business professionals who organized in 1964 to publish authoritative, timely books, information services, and journals written by specialists to assist accountants, tax practitioners, attorneys, and other business professionals; human resources, compensation and benefits, and pension and profit-sharing professionals; and owners of small- to medium-sized businesses. Our mission is to provide practical, solution-based "how-to" information to business professionals.

Also available in the Panel Answer Book series:

**Health Insurance Answer Book**
**The Pension Answer Book**
**Nonqualified Deferred Compensation Answer Book**
**Personnel Law Answer Book**
**Employee Assistance Law Answer Book**
**Employee Benefits Answer Book**

**PANEL PUBLISHERS, INC.**
**Practical Solutions for Business Professionals**

# Introduction

Panel's *Executive Compensation Answer Book* was specifically designed to meet the growing number of requests for a product that provides authoritative, practical guidance on how companies can structure executive compensation programs that not only help those companies to recruit, retain and motivate quality executives but also ensure that those companies receive the best return possible on their compensation dollar.

Companies fall into two broad compensation-related categories, those with informal and often unstated compensation policies and those with carefully conceived and communicated policies that are designed to meet the specific needs of the company. Unfortunately, there are a significant number of companies that have completely developed business plans and mission statements, but have not taken on the critical task of evaluating whether their executive compensation practices support their strategic, long-term goals and objectives. This is especially true in small, closely-held corporations where the management and ownership interests are substantially the same and there are no disinterested parties such as a Board of Directors to review and monitor the reasonableness of executive pay practices. However, it is critical to recognize the fact that no company is too small to have a formal compensation philosophy.

**How To Use This Book:** The *Executive Compensation Answer Book* is designed specifically for the business executive and professional advisor who need quick and authoritative answers to help them evaluate their company's executive compensation program and determine whether that program continues to meet the company's long-term goals. This book uses simple, straightforward language and avoids technical jargon whenever possible. Citations are provided as research aids whenever relevant for those who need to pursue a particular item in greater detail.

This book is divided into 11 chapters. Chapter 1 outlines the fundamental concepts of executive compensation and explains how the typical elements of an executive compensation package—base salary, annual incentives, long-term incentives, benefits, and per-quisites—can and should relate to each other when tailoring a compensation philosophy to your company's specific needs.

Chapter 2 covers the different considerations that must be addressed when developing a compensation plan for private companies versus public companies. This chapter is unique because it clearly recognizes that privately-held and closely-held companies, which are the most common form of small to medium-sized business ownership, have unique organizational characteristics that require a significantly different approach to executive compensation planning.

Chapter 3 covers base salary, which is the single largest element of a total compensation package. Because annual and long-term incentives are frequently developed as a percentage of base salary, this chapter is of critical importance because it clearly and concisely explains how to set an appropriate base salary as well as illustrates how an inappropriate base salary can compound the cost of a company's executive compensation program.

Chapter 4 deals with annual incentives, which are used to reward executives when a company or individual executive's performance meets or exceeds company expectations. The two major issues that predominate the implementation of an annual incentive program are (1) the degree that executive, business unit and company performance should impact the annual payout and (2) the performance measures that should be used to evaluate individual executive, business unit and company performance. This chapter explains how to use annual incentives, in what circumstances they work best, and the strengths and weaknesses of frequently used plans.

Chapter 5 provides an exhaustive overview of long-term incentive plans or capital accumulation accounts. It examines the issues that impact how long-term plans are designed and administered and explains the basic characteristics, similarities and differences between the three most common capital accumulation accounts:

1. Purchase plans;
2. Appreciation plans; and
3. Full-value plans.

Chapter 6 covers purchase plans, which are the most frequently used type of long-term incentive plan design. Purchase plans are intended to give an executive the opportunity to accumulate estate-building capital through the appreciation in the value of a company's stock or when other long-term company objectives are achieved. As the name implies, a purchase plan requires an executive to make an actual investment in the company by giving that executive the opportunity to purchase stock immediately or granting the executive options to purchase stock at a future date. This chapter covers the following types of purchase plans:

1. Incentive stock options (ISOs);
2. Nonstatutory options;
3. Restricted stock purchase plans;
4. Book value purchase plans;
5. Discounted nonstatutory options; and
6. Junior stock plans.

Chapter 7 covers the remaining two types of capital accumulation accounts, appreciation and full-value plans. The most common appreciation plan is the stock appreciation right (SAR) plan and the two most common types of full-value plans are incentive stock options (ISOs) and restricted stock grants (RSGs). This chapter addresses the various tax, legal and financial implications of these other common long-term incentive plans as well as the circumstances where they work best and the relative strengths and weaknesses of appreciation and full-value plans.

Chapter 8 covers combination long-term plans or tandem plans, which are plans that utilize more than one type of long-term incentive plan. This chapter covers the two most common combination plans, which are the phantom stock/stock option plan and the restricted stock/stock option plan although a third variation that is gaining in popularity, the contingent stock award, is also discussed.

Chapter 9 covers income deferral through the use of deferred compensation plans, which are playing an ever increasing role in total compensation packages for executives. The first major deferred compensation approach discussed in this chapter involves an agreement between an executive and a company for the executive to give up some portion of his or her current compensation package in return for the company's promise to make a deferred payment sometime in the future. Examples of this approach include top-hat plans (or Supplemental Executive Retirement Plans (SERPs)) and excess benefits plans. The second major approach does not include any income deferral but involves an additional future payment that is provided by the company to the executive. Examples of this approach include rabbi trusts and secular trusts. Finally, various other stock plans that can be established for the executive's benefit such as phantom stock are also covered.

Chapter 10 covers executive perquisites, which is the final component of a total compensation package. Although executive perquisites have lost most of their tax advantages in recent years, they still can provide strong psychological motivation for many executives at little cost to the company and remain an important element of an overall compensation program.

Finally, Chapter 11 deals with methods of compensating a company's board of directors. Historically, this issue was usually the concern of publicly-traded companies that needed to compensate a group of disinterested individuals for their efforts in monitoring corporate compensation practices, which is required by securities regulations. Today, however, even closely-held corporations are using outside directors to review and monitor their executive compensation decisions.

**Numbering System:** The questions are numbered consecutively within each chapter (e.g., 2:1, 2:2, etc.).

**Detailed Listing of Questions:** The detailed listing of questions that follows the table of contents at the front of the book is designed to help the reader locate specific areas of immediate interest. This listing functions as a detailed table of contents and provides the specific question that you are researching as well as the page number on which the answer appears.

**Glossary:** Because the executive compensation area is replete with technical terms that have specific legal meanings, a special glossary of terms is provided following the question-and-answer portion of the book. Expressions not defined elsewhere, and abbreviations used throughout the book, are defined in the glossary, which is arranged in alphabetical order.

**Index:** At the back of the book is a detailed key-word index that is provided as a further aid to locating specific topical information. All references in the Index are to question number rather than to page number.

Panel's *Executive Compensation Answer Book* is intended to provide you with a comprehensive set of answers to the issues you face when designing or evaluating your company's executive compensation philosophy. Using it in conjunction with Panel's highly acclaimed executive compensation survey report *Officer Compensation Report: The Executive Compensation Survey for Small to Medium- Sized Businesses* will allow you to compare your compensation practices with the actual pay practices of other companies within your industry to ensure that your company receives the best return on its compensation investment.

The Editors
December 1, 1991

# About the Authors

VYTENIS P. KURAITIS is a principal in the firm and the Midwest Practice Leader for Miller Mason & Dickenson's Compensation Practice based in Chicago. Prior to joining Miller Mason & Dickenson, Mr. Kuraitis spent nine years in consulting, most recently as Executive Compensation Practice Leader for a Big 6 accounting firm. Mr. Kuraitis also has 12 years experience as a corporate compensation professional with a focus on developing reward systems that reinforce corporate strategic plans or objectives. Mr. Kuraitis, a graduate of the University of Illinois, is a frequent speaker at professional organizations, is the author of numerous articles on compensation, performance appraisal and productivity and serves as the executive compensation columnist for Panel Publisher's *Compensation & Benefits Management.*

JANET AMBROSI WERTMAN, Esq., is an attorney with Davis & Gilbert in New York City, specializing in corporate and commercial practice. Through Davis & Gilbert, a law firm engaged in a full-service, general corporate, litigation, real estate, advertising and trademark practice, Ms. Ambrosi Wertman has extensive experience representing both employers and executives in employment situations. In addition, she has developed an expertise involving the day-to-day operational needs of a company as well as mergers and acquisitions and related issues. Prior to joining Davis & Gilbert, Ms. Ambrosi Wertman was an associate with Reavis & McGrath, also in New York City, in their corporate and securities law departments. Ms. Ambrosi Wertman, who is a member of the Business Law Section of the American Bar Association, received her B.A. degree from Barnard College of Columbia University and her J.D. degree from the Cornell Law School.

# Table of Contents

# Listing of Questions

## Chapter 1 Fundamental Concepts of Executive Compensation

# Chapter 2   Private Versus Public Company Considerations

# Chapter 3  Base Salary

# Chapter 4  Annual Incentives

# Chapter 5 Long-Term Incentive Plan Overview

# Chapter 6 Purchase Plans

# Chapter 7  Appreciation and Full-Value Plans

# Chapter 8 Combination Long-Term Plans

# Chapter 9 Income Deferral

## Tax Consequences to Employers and Employees

# Chapter 10 Perquisites and Other Benefits

# Chapter 11 Board of Directors' Compensation

# Chapter 1

# Fundamental Concepts of Executive Compensation

A crucial factor in the growth and development of a company is securing and retaining the service of quality executives. Efficiently designed executive compensation programs are an important ingredient in a company's ability to recruit and retain an executive team.

A typical executive compensation package consists of a base salary, annual incentives, long-term incentives, benefits, and perquisites. The cash components are the most easily measured and compared and tend to be where companies focus when trying to measure the competitiveness of their executives' pay. However, the cost to the company and the value to the executives of long-term incentives and executive benefits continue to grow.

The design of executive compensation packages is driven by competitive practices, tax and accounting rules and regulations, and company values and strategies. This chapter addresses the fundamental concepts in executive compensation.

### Q. 1:1  What is base salary?

Base salary is the amount of fixed cash compensation paid to the executive on a periodic basis (usually monthly or semi-monthly) that represents income that is not at risk. Most annual incentive programs and many capital accumulation plans are developed to produce a given payout that is thought of as a percentage of base salary. As a result, an uncompetitive base salary in most cases leads to uncompetitive annual incentive and capital accumulation programs unless the company's overall compensation philosophy is designed to use bonus programs to compensate for lower base salary.

### Q. 1:2   What is total compensation?

Total compensation is typically defined as the combination of base salary, annual incentives, long-term incentives, benefits and perquisites. Frequently this term is used to describe the components rather than the dollar amount because it is difficult to put a dollar value on the long-term incentive, benefits and perquisites components.

Each of the elements of the total compensation package meets a different executive need. Base salary provides the executive the cash to meet his or her day-to-day needs. Annual incentives supplement base salary (especially where base salary falls below comparable industry standards) and capital accumulation plans provide the executive with estate building capabilities. The benefit programs provide financial security in the case of death, disability, sickness or retirement while perquisites, such as club memberships, first class travel privileges, company cars are those special entitlements that are available only to a select group of executives.

# CEO Compensation Mix
## Survey of 100 Manufacturing Concerns

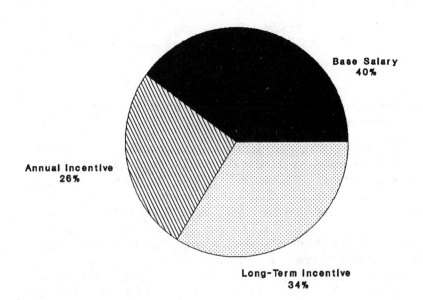

Base Salary
40%

Annual Incentive
26%

Long-Term Incentive
34%

Source: Miller Mason & Dickenson

## Q. 1:3 What are some of the factors that impact total compensation?

The following seven factors impact executive compensation:

- Type of responsibility;
- Level within organization;
- Type of industry;
- Supply and demand factors;
- Size of organization; and
- Executive performance

All other factors being constant, size of organization has the most significant impact on total compensation.

## Q. 1:4 Does the type of executive responsibilities impact total compensation?

Yes. The skills and responsibilities necessary to do the job and the types of achievements expected of the executive impact an executive's total compensation. For example, typically the Vice-President, Finance receives a higher total compensation than a Vice President of Human Resources because, in most companies, the Human Resources position is perceived as requiring fewer skills and responsibilities. Functional responsibility also greatly impacts an executive's base salary and there is a consistency between organizations as to how they view the "value" of functional responsibilities. As a percentage of the Chief Executive Officer's (CEO) total compensation, the total compensation packages for other executives who report to that CEO follow a fairly consistent pattern based on executive responsibilities.

The CEO's compensation is the foundation upon which the balance of a company's compensation practice rests. For this reason it is often useful to consider the relationship between the compensation of other executives and that of the CEO in determining general compensation structure. The following exhibit presents the unweighted average compensation of executive positions as a percentage of average CEO pay.

## BASE SALARY
### (As Percentage of CEO)

**All Manufacturing Companies by Company Size -**
**Chief Executive Officer/President**

Base Salary as of 4/1/91

| Annual Sales (millions $) | <2 | 2-5 | 5-10 | 10-15 | 15-25 | 25-40 | 40-60 | 60-100+ | Total |
|---|---|---|---|---|---|---|---|---|---|
| Average | 85 | 93 | 119 | 119 | 144 | 153 | 192 | 190 | 138 |
| Median | 75 | 85 | 110 | 118 | 138 | 150 | 180 | 178 | 130 |
| 1st Quartile | 47 | 68 | 93 | 100 | 108 | 130 | 146 | 150 | 95 |
| 3rd Quartile | 120 | 100 | 135 | 137 | 161 | 168 | 200 | 200 | 163 |
| 1990 Average | 79 | 87 | 112 | 113 | 136 | 142 | 173 | 181 | 130 |
| 90-91 % Change | 8% | 7% | 6% | 5% | 6% | 8% | 11% | 5% | 6% |

Base Salary as of 4/1/91 Incentive Program

| | <2 | 2-5 | 5-10 | 10-15 | 15-25 | 25-40 | 40-60 | 60-100+ | Total |
|---|---|---|---|---|---|---|---|---|---|
| Average | 84 | 91 | 121 | 120 | 139 | 150 | 194 | 186 | 143 |
| Median | 90 | 85 | 116 | 120 | 130 | 150 | 183 | 180 | 132 |
| 1st Quartile | 45 | 70 | 95 | 100 | 104 | 130 | 150 | 153 | 100 |
| 3rd Quartile | 100 | 98 | 138 | 137 | 160 | 165 | 200 | 200 | 168 |
| 1990 Average | 81 | 86 | 113 | 113 | 133 | 139 | 179 | 171 | 134 |
| 90-91 % Change | 4% | 6% | 7% | 6% | 5% | 8% | 8% | 9% | 7% |

Base Salary No Incentive Program

| | <2 | 2-5 | 5-10 | 10-15 | 15-25 | 25-40 | 40-60 | 60-100+ | Total |
|---|---|---|---|---|---|---|---|---|---|
| Average | 83 | 94 | 114 | 118 | 149 | 173 | 202 | 207 | 125 |
| Median | 60 | 85 | 108 | 120 | 137 | 156 | 166 | 170 | 108 |
| 1st Quartile | 47 | 65 | 89 | 90 | 108 | 125 | 92 | 140 | 85 |
| 3rd Quartile | 120 | 100 | 125 | 144 | 175 | 200 | 183 | 300 | 150 |
| 1990 Average | 75 | 90 | 110 | 117 | 138 | 164 | 155 | 226 | 117 |
| 90-91 % Change | 11% | 4% | 4% | 1% | 8% | 5% | 30% | -8% | 7% |

Short Term Incentive

| | <2 | 2-5 | 5-10 | 10-15 | 15-25 | 25-40 | 40-60 | 60-100+ | Total |
|---|---|---|---|---|---|---|---|---|---|
| % Eligible | 41% | 51% | 67% | 71% | 68% | 85% | 84% | 79% | 70% |
| % Paid | 27% | 78% | 68% | 79% | 73% | 83% | 76% | 70% | 74% |
| Avg. Bonus | 38 | 22 | 31 | 40 | 49 | 56 | 60 | 67 | 48 |
| 1991 Projected Avg. | 40 | 32 | 29 | 43 | 49 | 64 | 60 | 71 | 53 |
| 1991 Projected Median | 20 | 25 | 20 | 40 | 45 | 50 | 57 | 49 | 40 |

Total Cash Compensation

| | <2 | 2-5 | 5-10 | 10-15 | 15-25 | 25-40 | 40-60 | 60-100+ | Total |
|---|---|---|---|---|---|---|---|---|---|
| Average | 98 | 105 | 136 | 146 | 175 | 196 | 229 | 229 | 168 |
| Median | 90 | 98 | 122 | 145 | 173 | 181 | 218 | 200 | 152 |
| 1st Quartile | 52 | 79 | 100 | 110 | 136 | 154 | 183 | 175 | 108 |
| 3rd Quartile | 120 | 123 | 155 | 170 | 200 | 218 | 260 | 288 | 205 |

*Source: Growth Resource Officer Compensation Survey, 1991*

## TOTAL COMPENSATION
### (As Percentage of CEO)

**All Manufacturing Companies - Chief Executive Officer/President**

Officer Compensation As A Percentage of Chief Executive Compensation

| | Under 2 | | 2 - 5 | | 5 - 10 | | 10 - 15 | |
|---|---|---|---|---|---|---|---|---|
| | Base | Total | Base | Total | Base | Total | Base | Total |
| Chief Executive Officer/President | 100% | 100% | 100% | 100% | 100% | 100% | 100% | 100% |
| Chief Operating Officer | 87% | 86% | 72% | 70% | 77% | 76% | 83% | 78% |
| Top Subsidiary/Profit Ctr Executive | - | - | 89% | 84% | 68% | 67% | 68% | 64% |
| Top Administrative Executive | 58% | 54% | 59% | 57% | 62% | 60% | 65% | 58% |
| Top Sales & Marketing Executive | 78% | 71% | 67% | 69% | 62% | 58% | 67% | 62% |
| Top Sales Executive | 46% | 44% | 60% | 59% | 52% | 51% | 61% | 58% |
| Top Marketing Executive (No Sales) | - | - | 57% | 51% | 70% | 65% | 62% | 55% |
| Top Mfg/Prod Executive | 53% | 56% | 55% | 50% | 51% | 49% | 61% | 58% |
| Top Engineering Executive | 60% | 60% | 65% | 65% | 57% | 54% | 61% | 58% |
| Top R & D Executive | - | - | 71% | 70% | 69% | 68% | 76% | 71% |
| Top Quality Control Executive | - | - | 46% | 42% | - | - | 67% | 61% |
| Top Financial & Acctg Executive | 64% | 62% | 61% | 57% | 63% | 62% | 57% | 57% |
| Controller | 45% | 52% | 45% | 54% | 39% | 36% | 50% | 43% |
| Top Human Resources Executive | - | - | - | - | 43% | 38% | - | - |
| Top Purchasing Executive | - | - | 48% | 48% | - | - | - | - |
| Top MIS Executive | - | - | - | - | - | - | - | - |

*Source: Growth Resource Officer Compensation Survey, 1991*

### Q. 1:5  Does level within the organization impact an executive's total compensation?

Yes. The closer an executive's position is to the top position in the organization (usually the CEO), the more likely that the total compensation will be higher.

**Example:** The Vice President of Engineering in Company A reports to the Chief Operating Officer who in turn reports to the Chief Executive Officer. The Vice President of Engineering in Company B reports directly to the Chief Executive Officer. Assume that both companies have the same sales volume and the same number of employees. Consistently the Vice President of Engineering for Company B (who is closer in reporting structure to the CEO) will receive a higher base salary, a greater bonus eligibility, a more lucrative capital accumulation plan and probably have access to more perquisites. Part of this is caused by organization level salary differentials that most companies attempt to maintain. But, part of it is also caused by the organizational perspective that the closer an executive is to the CEO in reporting relationship, the more impact that executive has and, therefore, the greater his compensation should be.

### Q. 1:6  Does type of industry impact an executive's total compensation?

Yes. The industry in which an executive is employed has an impact on the total compensation of the executive because companies with larger sales volume or assets generally compensate their executives better (see Q. 1:8). Therefore, industries such as petroleum manufacturing and energy, which tend to be larger companies, provide higher compensation packages while banking, health care and insurance industries have traditionally been lower paying organizations.

**Planning Tip:** One way to decide on which industry or size of company your company needs or wants to be competitive with is to do an analysis to determine which companies or industries your current executives came from and where any former executives went to.

### Q. 1:7   Do supply and demand factors influence executive total compensation?

Yes. Because executive talent is a free market commodity, its price varies according to the classic laws of supply and demand. At various times during the past 30 years, financial executives have been more in demand than marketing executives while at other times during that same period of time, financial executives have been less in demand than marketing executives. This demand is created not only by the general economy and industry dynamics but also by the life cycle of a given company.

### Q. 1:8   Does company size influence total compensation?

Yes. Two CEO's with similar responsibilities will have different total compensation packages based solely on the size of organization. The executive in a company that has greater sales volume typically receives a higher base salary and because the annual incentive and stock awards are typically set as a percentage of base salary, the executive in a larger company will also receive, in absolute dollars, a larger incentive package.

Size does have an impact on establishing an executive's total compensation because organizational requirements and specifically, the need for salary differentials between organizational levels, leads large companies to pay more for executives. Consider a CEO of a $10 billion dollar company versus a CEO of a $1 billion dollar company. The CEO of the $10 billion company probably has a group Vice President who manages a $3 billion dollar business, who in turn has a division president who manages a $1 billion dollar business.

Note, however, that anchoring an executive's total compensation package on company size can create difficulties if a company is acquisition or divestiture oriented. If, from a corporate perspective, it makes sense to divest poor performing companies, does the company then reduce the CEO's salary each time it divests itself of a poorly performing company? Or, if the CEO acquires a subsidiary with large revenues but no profits, does the company automatically increase the CEO's salary?

### Q. 1:9   Does company performance impact total compensation levels?

If executive performance is measured in terms of company performance, there seems to be little correlation between that performance and base salaries and annual incentive amounts received. As a rule, salaries in successful firms as well as poorly performing firms tend to be the same. In fact, there is actually a tendency for salaries to be somewhat higher in companies performing poorly because of either the need to pay a high base salary to attract executives to a struggling company, or to compensate executives for incentive programs that don't actually pay out. On the other hand, annual incentive awards may be actively used to compensate for lower base salary amounts, which is the reverse of the situation in which base salary becomes inflated as a result of poorly designed annual incentive programs that have unrealistic payout standards. Where the annual incentive payout standards are properly designed, the company receives more for its compensation dollar because base salary can be set at or below market level while annual incentive payments reflect the company's (or individual executive's) performance.

However, annual incentive awards are still usually only slightly higher in successful firms than in unsuccessful firms, primarily because the unsuccessful firms tend to set low business performance targets. For example, a company with a historical profit margin of 2 percent may set its performance target at 3 percent while a company with a historical profit margin of 10 percent may set its performance goal at 15 percent. Assuming each company achieved its objectives, each probably would pay the same bonus amounts even though company performance varied significantly (i.e., 3 percent and 15 percent returns.)

Capital accumulation program payouts have a better correlation with how well the company performs because they are based on the appreciation of company's stock value. Therefore, payouts from these programs closely track the price appreciation of company stock. But, with stock option plans, the relationship between company performance and executive pay is not clear because the number of options granted and the absolute dollar values of the increases will have more impact on what an executive receives than does the percentage appreciation of the stock.

**Example:** Executive A in company Y receives an option to purchase 1,000 shares of stock at $5 per share. Executive B in company X receives an option to purchase 2,000 shares at $5. Executive C in company Z receives an option to purchase 2,000 shares at $6. All options are granted at the current market prices.

After five years, the stock for all three companies had appreciated 50%. Even though performance could be said to be the same at X, Y and Z, the executives would receive drastically different rewards. Executive A would receive a gain of $2,500 (New stock price $7.50 – option price $5 × 1,000 shares) while Executive B would receive $5,000 (New Stock price $7.50 – option price $5 × 2,000 shares), and Executive C would receive $6,000 (New Stock Price $9 – Option Price $6 × 2,000 shares). Stock appreciation was the same in percentage among the three companies, but Executive B had a higher reward than Executive A because he was granted a larger number of options; Executive C had a higher reward than Executive B because the dollar increase was larger.

## Q. 1:10   Does geographic location impact an executive base salary?

Surprisingly, no. As an example, it is generally argued that it costs more to live in New York City than in Cleveland, Ohio. However, when compensation levels for comparable positions in comparably sized organizations are compared, pay premiums for New York City are less than 10 percent, which is substantially less than the approximate 96 percent cost-of-living differential that exists between Cleveland and New York City.

Although there is little noticeable difference in total compensation packages for executives, geographic compensation differentials do occur among blue collar positions, white collar positions and lower to middle management.

In fact, the greatest impact of geographic and cost-of-living issues on executive compensation are the hiring bonuses for executives because companies based in high cost of living areas more frequently give hiring bonuses to compensate executives for entering a high cost-of-living area.

### Q. 1:11    How is base salary related to the other components of total compensation?

Both the annual incentive and the long-term incentive portions of the total compensation package are designed to generate a payout that is often calculated as a percentage of base salary although in many cases, adjustments to the annual and long-term incentive payouts are made to compensate for low base salary.

Where base salary is used as the foundation for the annual and long-term incentive portions it is important to note that acceptable deviations such as plus or minus 10 percent from the average base salary figure can create significant variations in total compensation for similarly situated executives. For example, assume a typical annual incentive for a CEO is 40 percent of base salary, and the annualized long-term plan goal is 20 percent and that the average salary for a CEO of a $200 million revenue size company is $200,000. Company A pays its CEO $180,000 (or 10% below market). Company B pays its CEO $220,000 (or 10% above market).

|  | Company A | Company B | Company C |
|---|---|---|---|
| Base | $180,000 | $220,000 | $200,000 |
| 40% Annual Incentive | 72,000 | 88,000 | 80,000 |
| 20% Long-Term | 36,000 | 44,000 | 40,000 |
|  | $288,000 | $352,000 | $320,000 |

Even though Company A places their executive at $20,000 or 10% below the average CEO market salary, an acceptable variation, Company A's executive actually receives $64,000 less in total compensation than company B's executive.

**Planning Tip:** When measuring how an executive compares to the market, you should consider total cost of the executive to the corporation. How that total cost compares is more meaningful than looking at individual components of the executive compensation package.

### Q. 1:12    What is the rationale for having an incentive plan?

There are several reasons why companies have incentive plans. First as a motivational tool because incentive payments have proven to be one of the most effective forms of compensation in terms of getting executives to focus on specific corporate performance objectives. Second, as a method to gain a comparative advantage or avoid a comparative disadvantage in terms of recruiting and retaining employees because so many companies today offer some sort of incentive plan to their executives, especially where base salary levels may be perceived as below the market rate. Third, to afford a measure of safety to the company in that as a variable form of compensation, incentive payments are reduced or eliminated as corporate performance declines. Also, the use of incentive payments may benefit the company's cash flow either because payments are "deferred" until the end of a year or because they are made in company stock.

Another rationale for having incentive plans is that if executives can make decisions and judgements that affect year-to-year company results, it makes sense for these executives to have a significant part of their current earnings dependent upon the achievement of these results.

### Q. 1:13   Are annual incentive plans appropriate for all types of organizations?

In those organizations where results are not quantifiable in dollars, annual incentive plans are difficult to implement and manage. Furthermore, annual incentive plans are usually not appropriate for most rapidly growing companies because it is difficult for these companies to set realistic goals on a year-to-year basis. However, the lack of an annual incentive plan in fast growth companies can typically be compensated for by lucrative long-term plans. Too often companies feel pressured to provide an annual incentive plan even though they are able to neither quantifiably measure performance nor establish quantifiable annual goals. As a result, these companies create plans that are nothing more than variable lump-sum base-salary payments. As such, companies facing these difficulties should consider increasing base salaries and/or long-term incentive opportunities.

### Q. 1:14  What characteristics identify organizations for which annual incentive plans are feasible?

There are several characteristics that identify those companies and/or industries for which incentive plans are more feasible.

The first is the situation where numerous short-term decisions impact company profits. In this case, key profit influencing decisions tend to be short-term and the success of a decision can be judged in a relatively short period of time (i.e., one year or less).

The second is where the organization is decentralized. Executives have clearly defined areas of profit and loss responsibility and individuals, not committees, have authority to make decisions and implement them.

The third is where the accounting and economic data used to evaluate performance is available and accessible. Too often, this characteristic is overlooked.

The fourth characteristic is a management team that is demanding of their executive group because these types of companies create a management attitude that focuses on results.

Finally, a fifth characteristic is where base salary is set below market level but annual incentives are used to compensate for the variance.

### Q. 1:15  How can companies deal with executives' focusing on the short-run at the expense of long-term performance in their efforts to receive high annual payout?

Annual incentives can create an overemphasis on short-term performance. However if the executive's performance objectives have given him or her the opportunity to "mortgage the future" for current reward, the performance objectives are faulty. A well thought-out, balanced list of objectives should preclude the possibility of such a course of action by the executive.

**Planning Tip:** One plan design method of ensuring that executives do not overemphasize annual performance is to make sure that the sum of the annual rewards over a period of time is less than the probable long-term plan payout. Consider a CEO who is currently earning a base salary of $200,000 and is eligible for an annual incentive plan payment of 50 percent of that base and is also eligible for a long-term plan that will pay out in five years.

| Year | Base* | Annual Incentive |
|------|-------|------------------|
| 1992 | $200,000 | $100,000 |
| 1993 | 214,000 | 107,000 |
| 1994 | 228,980 | 114,490 |
| 1995 | 245,008 | 122,504 |
| 1996 | 262,158 | 131,079 |

*Assume 7% annual salary adjustment.

The long-term plan should be designed so that if performance expectations are met both on an annual and long-term basis, the long-term plan should pay out at least $575,073 (sum of annual incentive payouts) and probably 150 percent of that amount, or $862,609. With such a large long-term payout, the financial incentive will weigh towards the long-term.

## Q. 1:16   What is the typical relationship between annual and long-term incentives?

Most companies claim to focus on the long-run performance of their executives. But except for chief executive officer positions, most executives receive more from the sum of their annual incentive plans than they do under long-term incentive plans.

## Q. 1:17   What are some basic guidelines for incentive plan design?

Obviously, all incentive plans must be tailored to the company's policies and to its financial and operating circumstances. To help focus on these issues, many companies develop a written compensation philosophy statement (See Q. 1:20). This statement, which documents the values and the unique operating circumstances of the company as they relate to the compensation of executives, can be used as a measure in the development of incentive programs. For example if a company's compensation philosophy states that the organization values team work and group performance, it clearly would be inappropriate to develop an incentive program emphasizing individual performance.

### Q. 1:18    Typically, who is eligible for incentive plan participation?

There is a great variance between companies and within industries on what percentage of executives participate in an annual incentive plan. However, as a rough rule of thumb, 2 percent of employees in an organization are eligible to participate. One principal factor affecting the extent of eligibility in incentive plans is whether the company is capital intensive or people intensive. Highly capital intensive industries have proportionately fewer individuals eligible for incentive plans.

Companies should consider two primary factors when determining eligibility for incentive plans. First, they should include those executives who can make decisions that affect the results of the company overall or in its business units in a significant way. Second, companies should also consider competitive practices. If there are positions that normally participate in incentive plans in other organizations, then these position must be closely scrutinized for participation.

In most cases, eligibility is somewhat arbitrary, but is typically based on one or more of the following criteria:

1. Salary level, for example "all employees who earn $60,000 or more per year";
2. Salary grade, for example, "all employees who are in compensation grade 20 or higher";
3. Organizational level, for example "all executives who report directly to the Chief Executive or Chief Operating Officer";
4. Combination approaches, for example "all executives who are in grade 20 or higher and report directly to the Chief Executive or Chief Operating Officer."

Each of these approaches has distinct disadvantages. Earnings level favors those disciplines with high market worth and may not reflect potential impact on the company performance. Salary grade cutoff favors the market value considerations that went into designing the salary structure. Finally, the organizational level approach can easily be subject to tampering and result in the inclusion of executives with relatively minor responsibilities while excluding those executives who have substantial organizational impact.

**Planning Tip:** To determine whether an executive should be eligible for an annual incentive program, write down three responsibilities and the corresponding results that are measurable and will have substantial negative or positive impact on the company. If you can't come up with a list of three, the executive shouldn't be eligible for an incentive.

### Q. 1:19 How do executive compensation programs differ in emerging or start-up companies?

Stock-based plans are a common component of an executive compensation program for executives in both young and mature companies. Stock-based plans are even more crucial to start-up and emerging companies because many start-up companies and emerging companies cannot offer competitive base salary and benefits to executives. In addition, annual incentive plans that pay out in cash can be large cash drains to a start-up company.

The start-up or emerging company can, however, offer something that the mature company may not be able to offer: a chance for the executive to build wealth through stock ownership, if and when the company succeeds. This is particularly common in the field of high technology where it is common for stock-based compensation to be a significant part of the total package. Often this package is offered not only to executives, but to other key managers and technical staff as well.

### Q. 1:20 How does corporate philosophy affect the method of compensation chosen?

Traditionally, companies have focused on the external market to determine their executive compensation plan design. Base salary levels, long and short-term incentive eligibility levels, and incentive plan payout amounts were primarily determined by what the competition was doing. As a result, base salaries tended to become inflated to compensate for poorly designed annual incentive plan payouts. While these competitive issues are important, they should not be used to the exclusion of the company's compensation philosophy, which states the operating and organizational values that impact compensation.

For example, a company needs to address issues such as:

- How much compensation should be at risk?
- Should organization levels affect how much compensation is at risk?
- How competitive does the organization want or need to be?

These internal organizational values, expressed in a compensation philosophy statement, should be as important as competitive issues in determining the appropriate design of an executive compensation program.

**Planning Tip:** Distribute on an annual basis, your company's corporate compensation philosophy to your top executives and members of the Board of Directors, to generate the development of new programs on this agreed upon philosophy.

### Q. 1:21   What are the general tax implications of different forms of compensation?

As a general rule, amounts paid by companies to their employees as compensation are tax deductible to the company, as long as certain requirements are met. These requirements are:

1. The compensation must be an ordinary and necessary business expense;
2. The compensation must be reasonable in amount; and
3. In the case of personal services, the compensation must be paid in the taxable year the services are actually rendered.

The timing of the compensation deduction may be affected by whether the company uses the cash or accrual method of accounting. For a cash-basis company, all amounts paid to employees are deductible as and when the payments are actually made to the employees. For an accrual-basis company, amounts paid to employees are deductible as and when the obligation to make the payments accrues, that is, when the liability for payment is fixed and definite and not subject to indeterminable future events.

From the executive's point of view, he or she will in all likelihood recognize income in the year in which he or she receives the payment, even if the company is able to deduct the payment in a different year. However, some individuals may elect to be taxed on an accrual basis and these individuals will recognize income in the year in which it accrues.

### Q. 1:22   What is unreasonable compensation?

The compensation package of key executives must be reasonable to be deductible by the company. In determining reasonableness, the Internal Revenue Service ("IRS") considers a number of key factors including:

- Compensation paid to executives in similar jobs in similar organizations;
- Executive qualifications, such as previous experience and academic credentials;
- Size and complexity of the business; and
- Executive duties.

The IRS will also take into account the nature of the compensation in determining whether it is reasonable. Incentive compensation, which is usually compensation that is contingent on the company's future performance, can generally be given in amounts that would be considered unreasonable if paid to the executive in the form of salary. This is because the executive is risking part of his compensation based upon the company's performance and should be entitled to a greater reward based on that performance.

Questions regarding the reasonableness of compensation most often arise in connection with payments made to shareholder-executives of a closely-held corporation (see Q. 2:12), especially where those shareholder-executives own a substantial part of the stock of their employer. This is because it is unclear in this situation whether the compensation is actually a disguised distribution of profits rather than true compensation. Therefore, IRS closely scrutinizes situations where compensation or bonuses are proportionate to the amount of stock owned and/or where the company is generating profits but paying nominal or no dividends to its shareholders.

### Q. 1:23   What happens if an executive's compensation is deemed "unreasonable"?

If IRS determines that the compensation paid to an executive, including deferred and incentive compensation, is unreasonable, the alleged excess will not be deductible to the company unless the company is able to prove that the compensation is in fact reasonable. The executive, of course, would be taxed on the amounts received, whether or not deductible by the company.

Where IRS disallows a compensation deduction, the company could request or require the repayment by the executive of the amounts that were not deductible. Some companies require executives to sign a formal document to this effect before they will make any substantial compensation payments. Such repayment agreements are often referred to as "hedge agreements" or "Oswald agreements." However, the existence of such an arrangement implies that the company believed that the compensation was in fact unreasonable and may tip the scales against the company in the event of an IRS investigation.

### Q. 1:24   What is ordinary income?

Ordinary income is reportable income that does not qualify as capital gains.

### Q. 1:25   What are capital gains?

Before 1987, preferential long-term capital gain treatment was accorded to profits from the sale of certain types of property that had been held by the owner for at least 6 months. The favorable long-term capital gains rules provided for a deduction equal to 60 percent of the net capital gain that resulted from the sale. Currently capital gains are taxed at only a slight differential from ordinary income.

### Q. 1:26   What was the rationale for favorable capital gains treatment?

The capital gains treatment had been intended to encourage risk taking by investors. In addition, it was, in part, a recognition that appreciation in value over a long period should not be taxed in full in the year of the income receipt. Because of the substantial reduction in tax rates provided by the Tax Reform Act of 1986 (TRA '86), Congress concluded that it was no longer necessary to provide preferential treatment for capital gains, although it recently provided for a small differential in the capital gains rate.

### Q. 1:27    How does the lack of capital gains treatment impact executive compensation planning?

The repeal of the capital gains deduction is having a significant and positive impact on executive compensation programs. In prior periods, because of the tax advantages of certain executive pay vehicles, the emphasis in plan design was on the tax advantages rather than corporate strategies or objectives. If the programs provided tax breaks to the company and/or executives, the programs were deemed good regardless of whether shareholder wealth was increased or executive ownership objectives were supported. With the passing of many of the tax advantages, the focus has returned to programs that reinforce corporate objectives and strategies. Vehicles such as incentive stock options, book-value stock and convertible debentures, which have a goal of converting compensation income (i.e., ordinary income) to capital gains, become less attractive when those gains are taxed at ordinary income rates, particularly where the company loses the right to claim a deduction and the individual may become subject to a preference tax on the benefit.

### Q. 1:28    What is the effective tax rate?

The effective tax rate is the rate the executive pays on all of his or her taxable income. For example, if the executive's taxable income was $200,000 and the tax bill was $40,000, the effective tax rate is 20 percent.

### Q. 1:29    What is the marginal tax rate?

The marginal tax rate is the rate the executive pays on the last dollar that is earned. The knowledge of an executive's marginal tax rate helps to calculate how much a tax deduction is worth to the executive. For example, if an executive's marginal tax rate is 28 percent, a $1,000 deduction saves the executive $280 in tax.

### Q. 1:30   What is the alternative minimum tax?

The alternative minimum tax (AMT) is a second method of calculating an executive's tax liability. The AMT is sometimes called the "add-back tax," because the calculation of the AMT involves adding back adjustments and tax preferences and then subtracting deductions that are allowed under the AMT. The AMT is designed to ensure that all high income level executives bear at least a minimum level of the federal tax burden. An executive must use the AMT calculation to determine taxes due when primary sources of income are tax sheltered or subject to favorable tax treatment. Such situations may occur when a large portion of income has been realized through stock option gains or certain tax sheltered investments, or where a large portion of income has been protected by tax shelters.

The AMT requires that an affected executive calculate his or her tax liability without excluding his or her tax preference items. If this tax liability (currently 21 percent of taxable income) is less than the regular tax liability, the executive is liable for additional tax.

# Chapter 2

# Private Versus Public Company Considerations

Privately-held and closely-held companies have unique organizational characteristics that typically require a significantly different approach to executive compensation. Frequently, an executive compensation plan that is effective and appropriate in publicly-traded organizations will be neither effective nor appropriate in a privately-held company. The use of stock-based plans, for instance, so common in publicly-traded companies is less extensive in private companies. Furthermore, in small start-up companies, annual incentive plans that are so common in large organizations are difficult to make effective.

The chapter addresses the private company considerations as compared to public company considerations in the design of executive compensation programs as well as plan design and competitive practices.

### Q. 2:1　What is a "public" or "publicly-traded" company?

A company is "publicly traded" if it has a class of equity securities that are registered under the Securities Exchange Act of 1934 (the "1934 Act") and, as a result, is subject to the ongoing disclosure and reporting requirements of the 1934 Act.

Equity securities must be registered under the 1934 Act if either a public offering of those securities is made under the Securities Act of

1933 (the "1933 Act"), or if the company in question has more than $3 million in total assets or more than 500 shareholders of any one class of its equity securities.

### Q. 2:2  What is a "private" or "privately-held" company?

A company is "privately-held" if none of its equity securities are registered under the 1934 Act.

### Q. 2:3  What is a closely-held company?

A closely-held company is one in which management and owner-ship are substantially the same. The term "closely-held corporation" is derived from the fact that the company's stock is "held closely" by a few individuals. Such companies are frequently referred to as "close corporations" or "family corporations."

### Q. 2:4  Is a "privately-held" company always considered "closely-held" as well?

No, although these terms are often incorrectly used interchan-geably. A "closely-held" company will always be a "privately-held" company.

### Q. 2:5  Do executive compensation programs in privately-held companies differ from executive compensation programs in publicly-traded companies?

Yes, because the underlying motivations of compensation pro-grams differ from public to private companies. A public company's primary motivation in instituting a compensation program is to offer executives enough compensation to make them remain with the company and motivate them to work their hardest toward achieving the company's strategic interests. This motivation exists already for owner-executives of a private company because they already have a substantial stake in the company's profits and, therefore, in ensuring the company achieves its strategic interests. As a result, a private company will concentrate on rewarding its owner-executives for their efforts through compensation that is tax-deductible to the company rather than by simply increasing profits, which would then have to be paid to the same owner-executives through taxable corporate dividends.

**Practice Pointer:** In large privately-held companies, base salaries for executives appear to be somewhat higher. This may reflect the limited capital accumulation opportunities and the career caps that exist in closely-held companies. The career caps reflect the fact that in many privately-held companies, the top positions are available only to the family members of the primary owners.

On the other hand, annual incentive plans in privately-held companies do not significantly differ in design from those in publicly-traded companies. The design of the programs is not significantly different from publicly traded companies. However, privately-held companies tend to place more emphasis on internally set objectives rather than peer comparisons, and cash flow, return on investment and book value growth appear frequently as performance measures for these companies.

# Privately Held Company
## Long-Term Incentive Plans

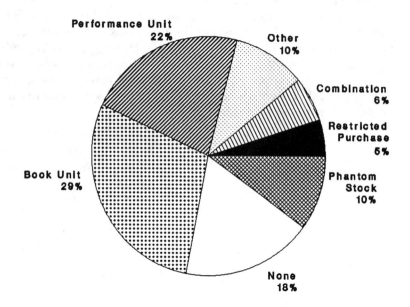

**Source: Miller Mason & Dickenson, 1990**

### Q. 2:6   Do privately-held companies use stock-based capital accumulation programs to structure their executive compensation arrangements?

Rarely, because it is valueless to grant stock to owners, especially in proportion to their current ownership interests, and the owners generally do not wish to widely grant options to their non-owner employees because they do not want to substantially increase the number of owners. If a privately-held company does use a stock based capital accumulation program, it tends to not distribute the stock options or restricted stock as widely as would be the case in a publicly traded company. Furthermore, the private company would certainly be well advised to keep the number of shareholders comfortably below the 500 number, which would prevent triggering the reporting requirements under the 1934 Act.

### Q. 2:7   Why wouldn't a privately-held company use stock options for executive compensation plans?

There are several reasons why stock option plans and stock based plans are used less frequently in privately-held companies. One reason, as stated above, is that an executive compensation plan that uses stock eventually results in a minority shareholder position for a number of executives, with all the rights that this position entails, including the right to vote stock, review financial records and attend shareholder meetings. This may not be appealing to the majority owners, both because their ownership becomes diluted and because they have additional people to "answer" to. In addition, this minority ownership can lead to an unfriendly minority shareholder if the executive is terminated or leaves the firm to join a competitor, although this problem may be avoided through the use of restrictive buy-back agreements. These agreements typically obligate executives to sell their stock back to the company or the majority shareholder following termination of employment or allow currently-employed executives to liquidate their investment. These agreements also typically allow the buy-back to take place over a reasonable span of time to avoid the cash burden to the company owners that could result from an obligation to immediately purchase the stock.

Another reason that privately-held companies may avoid the use of stock-based plans is the problem of valuing the stock for establishing the purchase price. As a result, the buy-back agreement usually stipulates a formula price or method by which the purchase price is to be determined at the time of sale.

### Q. 2:8　How do privately-held companies that use stock as a compensation mechanism structure their executive compensation arrangements?

The most frequently used capital accumulation plans in closely held companies are book value plans (see Q. 6:50) performance units plans (see Q. 7:33) and phantom stock plans (see Q. 7:14). If stock based plans are offered, they are almost always accompanied by buy-back provisions.

### Q. 2:9　Is there an effect if a privately-held company does not provide capital accumulation plans?

Yes. In not providing capital accumulation programs, privately-held companies are denying themselves an important tool to recruit, retain and direct executive talent. They also are probably paying more than is necessary in fixed cash compensation. In addition, they are losing the opportunity to put executives in the same boat as the owners.

Virtually all types of privately-held companies can offer meaningful capital accumulation plans to key executives, the most prevalent type of which is a cash-based long-term phantom stock plan.

**Practice Pointer:** A less common capital accumulation approach is the use of a true stock-based plan. These plans can be exactly like those used by publicly-traded companies, with an exception: Executives are able to sell their shares only to the company, which is typically enforced by granting the company a right of first refusal. The company may also want to specify financing terms as part of the repurchase agreement, permitting it to settle the executive's interests over a number of years to minimize the impact of an immediate cash drain.

### Q. 2:10   What is a Subchapter S corporation?

The Internal Revenue Code (the "Code") permits shareholders of certain privately-held companies to elect to be taxed as though the shareholders were carrying on their activities as partners. In such a case, the shareholders are taxed directly on the earnings of the company in proportion to their ownership of stock. As a result of this election, the shareholders avoid the double taxation of corporate earnings (first, at the corporate level on the company's earnings and, second, at the individual level when those earnings are distributed to the shareholders in the form of dividends) by passing the tax obligations through to themselves.

### Q. 2:11   How does a company elect to become a Subchapter S corporation?

A corporation becomes a Subchapter S corporation (S corporation) by filing an S Corporation election under Code Section 1362(a). That election may only be made by a corporation that meets the following eligibility requirements:

1. It must be a corporation organized under the laws of the United States;
2. It cannot have more than 35 shareholders;
3. Its shareholders must be either individuals, estates or certain trusts; and
4. It cannot have more than one class of stock.

Furthermore, certain types of companies are ineligible for S corporation treatment whether or not they meet the above criteria. Such companies include financial institutions, insurance companies, and members of an affiliated group as determined under Code Section 1504(b). Generally, the most significant implication of the "affiliated group" prohibition is that an S corporation may not have a subsidiary unless another person or entity holds at least 20 percent of the total voting power and also holds a value equal to at least 20 percent of the total value of the subsidiary's stock, or unless that subsidiary is in fact inactive.

### Q. 2:12   Does electing S corporation status have an impact on executive compensation?

Yes. An S corporation must be very careful in implementing a stock-based plan because of the risk of losing its S corporation status as a result of a violation of one of the eligibility requirements (see Q. 2:10). First, the number of executives entitled to participate must be limited because an S corporation cannot have more than 35 shareholders. Second, the plans must be monitored to ensure that they do not, by design or unintentionally, create a second class of stock.

The events that create a second class of stock are not always clear. For example, capital accumulation plans utilizing warrants or convertible debentures have been found to constitute a second class of stock, while the creation of a class of non-voting stock has been found *not* to be a second class of stock. The use of restricted shares may constitute a second class of stock where shares that are issued are subject to such substantial conditions or restrictions that they are deemed to not have the same rights to corporate assets as other unrestricted, company stock. Nevertheless, certain restrictions can be imposed *without* creating a second class of stock. Such restrictions include:

- Requiring the executive to obtain corporate consent prior to selling the shares to a third party;
- Requiring the executive to resell the shares to the company at a specified price, even if that price is less than the fair market value of the shares; and
- Providing that the executive will forfeit the shares if he or she quits or is fired for good cause.

Typically, an S corporation will choose to avoid the problems associated with stock-based plans by using related devices such as Stock Appreciations Rights (SARs) and Phantom Stock Plans.

The election of S corporation status also has an impact on the adoption of other nonqualified deferred compensation vehicles such as rabbi trusts or corporate owned life insurance although these vehicles are rarely used by S corporations because they have little value to the owner-executive of an S corporation. The reason they are of little value is because the S corporation is not a tax-shielding entity like a regular corporation is. As a result, the owner-executives are currently taxed, like partners, on the income held by the company or paid in the form of insurance premiums.

### Q. 2:13 Does the issue of "unreasonable compensation" affect publicly-traded companies differently than it does privately-held and S corporations?

Technically no; in practice, yes. The requirement that compensation be reasonable applies universally to all companies. There is nothing in the Code or corresponding Treasury Regulations (regulations) that limits the application of unreasonable compensation issues to privately-held companies. However, in practice, it is almost exclusively the privately-held company that is challenged on this issue. The reason for this seemingly selective application is that there is far greater potential for and likelihood of abuse in the case of a privately-held company where the owner-executives have the power to fix their own compensation and to control the company's dividend paying policy. Furthermore, the requirement that a publicly-traded corporation discloses the amount of profits it earns each year as well as the compensation it pays to its top executives, acts as a natural barrier against the payment of excessive salaries.

S corporations, although privately-held, are generally exempt from this special scrutiny because there is no reason for the owner-executives to try to recharacterize dividend payments as compensation unless the compensation in question is of a type (e.g., retirement plan contributions or deferred compensation) that affects the company's tax situation. However, the S corporation situation creates the mirror image of the unreasonable compensation issue: The owner-executive of an S corporation will tend to recharacterize salary as dividends in order to avoid the federal unemployment taxes, Social Security (FICA) taxes and the federal withholding tax requirements that are applicable to compensation payments.

Regardless of the type of company involved, several general principles apply. First, the IRS determination of unreasonable compensation is presumed to be correct. Therefore, if IRS determines that the compensation is unreasonable, the burden of proving that the payments are reasonable falls on the company. Second, in any compensation arrangement between a privately-held company and its owner-executives, it is assumed that there is an absence of arm's-length bargaining, which increases the likelihood that compensation will be found to be unreasonable. Third, each case is decided on its own facts. This is generally seen as a principle that is more favorable to the executive and the company because it gives more latitude to each company. Unfortunately, as a result, there are no firm guidelines or precedents to rely on in analyzing a reasonable compensation issue because each company, executive and situation is different.

**Q. 2:14**    **What is the Securities Act of 1933 and the Securities Exchange Act of 1934 and how do they impact executive compensation?**

The 1933 Act and the 1934 Act, and the regulations promulgated under these Acts, set forth the principal federal rules governing the issuance and sale of securities in the United States. The 1933 Act governs the sale by a company of shares of its stock to the public while the 1934 Act sets forth various obligations on companies whose shares are held by the public. Both Acts are guided by the general principle that a company may operate as it sees fit as long as it discloses all pertinent information to its shareholders.

Under the 1933 Act, every offer and sale of a security must be registered with the Securities and Exchange Commission (the "SEC") unless the offer and sale are exempt from registration. There is a "private offering" exemption for offerings not made to the general public as well as an exemption for certain offers and sales of securities by private companies that are made pursuant to employee benefit plans or contracts its employees, consultants or advisors. Rule 144 under the 1933 Act allows the executive of a public company to hold securities which have not been registered under the 1933 Act, also known as "restricted securities," for a minimum of two years, at which time the executive may re-sell the shares to the public subject to the volume limitation and other manner-of-sale requirements of Rule 144. After the securities have been held for three years, they may be transferred without regard to the volume limitations.

From a practical point of view, the executive who is not deemed to be an "affiliate" of a publicly-traded company (that is, an executive who does not control that company) will often be unaffected by the 1933 Act because the company will have registered the shares of stock that it grants through its employee benefit and option plans on a Form

S-8 registration statement (see Q. 2:21) and may therefore be resold without concern. Similarly, the executive of a privately-held company will often be unaffected by the 1933 Act because shares granted will usually be subject to the requirement that they be resold to the company.

The 1934 Act contains the reporting rules that must be followed by a company whose shares are held by the public. The basic principle is that everyone who buys and sells shares of the company's stock must have access to the same information concerning the company at the same time. This principle prevents certain categories of people, referred to as "insiders," from profiting at the public's expense from any information that they have gained solely by reason of their position with the company. Therefore, a publicly-traded company must file quarterly and annual statements containing audited financial statements and must notify the public of any material changes in its business or operations. Furthermore, the publicly-traded company's executive officers and directors are prohibited from buying or selling shares of company stock if they have any material information that has not yet been disclosed to the public.

The 1934 Act's primary effects on executive compensation arise from the fact that the company must disclose the compensation paid each year to its most highly compensated employees and from the presumption set forth in Section 16 and the rules promulgated under that Section that an insider who buys and sells stock in a six-month period is trading on inside information.

### Q. 2:15   What are the basic Section 16 rules?

Section 16 of the 1934 Act is designed to minimize the unfair use of "inside information," which is information that is not available to the public. This is accomplished through the interaction of Section 16(a), under which an "insider" must promptly disclose all his transactions in company stock, and Section 16(b), under which any profits made by an insider from transactions involving a purchase and sale of company stock within any six-month period must be returned to the company. Any combination of purchase and sale within the six-month period will result in a violation of Section 16(b), regardless of how long the shares being sold have been held or whether the executive was in fact in possession of material non-public information.

In determining the amount of profit earned, the rules utilize the calculation that will produce the highest recovery for the company. That is, the highest sale price will be matched with the lowest purchase price in the period.

The SEC has recognized that the participation by executives in certain employee benefits plans is not the type of situation that is particularly subject to abuse of inside information. As a result, certain transactions within those plans are exempt from the application of the Section 16 rules. These exemptions were recently changed and an analysis of the changes appears at Question 2:16.

### Q. 2:16  What were the major changes in the Section 16 rules effective May 1, 1991?

The new Section 16 rules changed the definition of who was an insider slightly and now bring directors, executive officers and holders of 10 percent or more of the outstanding shares of a company's stock under Section 16. The term "executive officers" includes "presidents or vice-presidents who are in charge of a principal business unit, division or function, and other persons who perform similar policy-making functions." (Note 33 to Release No 34-28869) Specifically included in this category are the company's principal financial officer and principal accounting officer or controller. Executive officers of parent or subsidiary companies can also be considered executive officers of the company itself if they perform the described functions. The new definition is narrower than the previous definition, which subjected all officers, regardless of policy-making function, to the reporting requirements and potential liability of Section 16.

The definition of 10 percent owner has changed in some minor respects; it is now tied directly to the definition provided in Section 13(d) of the 1933 Act. Essentially, the opportunity, directly or indirectly, to profit or share in the applicable transaction, or the right to vote or direct the voting of shares, constitutes ownership of the shares.

The new Section 16(a) reporting requirements are similar to the old ones. Under the new requirements, an insider files a Form 3 at the time he or she becomes an insider setting forth the number of shares of company stock then owned by the insider (including shares held by spouses, children, and any other relative living in the insider's household), as well as the number of shares the insider is then entitled to acquire upon the exercise of any option or other right. Any changes are then reported on a Form 4 within the first 10 days of the month following the month in which the transaction took place, except for the changes that are exempt from Section 16(b) liability, which may be voluntarily reported immediately, but otherwise are to be reported on the first Form 4 that the insider is otherwise required to file or on a Form 5 filed within 45 days after the end of the year. An important new "sanction" contained in Section 16(a) is the obligation of the company to report in the annual information that it provides to its shareholders, not only any violations by any of its insiders of the short-swing profit rules of Section 16, but also any lapses or mistakes in the filing of the disclosure reports.

One of the most significant changes to Section 16(b) involves the treatment of the acquisition and exercise of options and other derivative securities. Under the new rules, the acquisition of an option, warrant or other convertible security is deemed to be the equivalent of the acquisition of the underlying common stock. However, the exercise of the option or warrant or conversion of the convertible security will not be a purchase or sale of the underlying securities for purposes of Section 16 except where the exercise is of an out-of-the-money option. These rules are discussed extensively in Chapter 5.

Rule 16b-3 continues to provide guidelines for certain employee benefit plans, including stock option plans, where participation is not deemed to be subject to the abuse of insider information. As long as these plans meet the 16b-3 guidelines, grants of options and other securities will not be deemed to be purchases of the securities for purposes of Section 16(b) although they will be subject to Section 16(a) reporting requirements.

### Q. 2:17   What are the most significant effects of the new Section 16 rules from a compensation perspective?

The revised rules that exempt the exercise of an option from the liability provision of Section 16 allow an executive to exercise an option and sell shares of stock (to pay for that exercise) simultaneously. As a result, many compensation devices designed to provide the executive with cash to exercise his options, such as tandem plans, are no longer necessary and many other devices designed to avoid the scope of Section 16 while providing similar benefits, such as cash-settled SARs, are no longer desirable.

From a corporate perspective, employee benefits plans may have to be amended in order to comply with the revised Section 16 exemption requirements. These technical aspects are an effect of the revised rules that should not be overlooked.

### Q. 2:18   What is a shareholder proxy and proxy statement?

A shareholder's proxy is his authorization to vote his shares at a meeting in his place in accordance with his instructions. The proxy method was developed because of the difficulties that would be involved if all shareholders had to vote directly on corporate matters, including the annual election of directors. The 1934 Act regulates the solicitation of proxies for public companies by requiring that the shareholder be furnished with enough information to make an informed decision regarding the vote he casts. Section 14 of the 1934 Act specifies that no proxy may be solicited without being preceded or accompanied by a proxy statement. The contents of the proxy statement depend on the vote sought. For example, if a proxy is sought for the election of directors, or if shareholder approval is sought in connection with any stock option, incentive, profit sharing, pension or other compensation plan in which officers are to participate, the proxy statement must disclose, among other things, the compensation paid to the company's most highly compensated executive officers, including amounts paid pursuant to any benefit and stock option plans.

### Q. 2:19   How does the reporting requirement affect executive compensation?

The requirement that a company disclose to its shareholders and the public each year the amounts it has paid to its most highly compensated executives is generally believed to act as a limitation on executives' salaries. The shareholders can always initiate a derivative action in court to challenge the amounts or kinds of compensation afforded to executives independently of an IRS challenge of that compensation as unreasonable. Although the actual shareholder challenges to compensation are rarely successful, especially where a disinterested committee is involved in determining compensation, executives appear to be just as fearful of the press these challenges generate and the image of waste they allege, as well as the perceived invitation caused by the waste to a hostile takeover attempt.

### Q. 2:20   What is the Compensation Committee of the Board and what role does it play in executive compensation?

The Compensation Committee of the Board is a specially designated committee of the Board of Directors, generally composed of a company's outside, disinterested directors. Where it exists, the Compensation Committee is the entity that administers the employee benefit plans and determines the employees who will receive options or other securities, and in what amounts. (The use of outside directors and special compensation plans for them is more fully discussed in Chapter 11.)

### Q. 2:21   How do the new S-8 rules affect executive compensation?

Form S-8 is the registration form that is used by a company to register under the 1933 Act those shares of its stock issuable pursuant to its benefit plans. Recent revisions to the rules have significantly eased the procedures. First, the new rules simplified the format to make the actual registration easier. Second, the new rules also extended the use of Form S-8 to allow companies to register shares to be granted as compensation to consultants or advisors and not just options to be granted to actual employees.

The S-8 registration exempts only the "sale" by the company. At the next stage, executives who are not affiliates of the company may resell the shares in normal broker transactions. Executives who are affiliates of the company may resell the shares either by using a tandem reoffer prospectus or under the volume limitations (but not the holding period requirement) of Rule 144.

# Chapter 3

# Base Salary

Base salary represents the single largest element of the total compensation package, which consists of salary, annual and long-term incentives, benefits and perquisites. Base salary is still the principal method of compensating executives. Because annual and long-term incentives are frequently developed as a percentage of base salary, an inappropriate base salary can have a compounding effect on the total executive pay plan.

From a business standpoint, the ideal base salary is the one that, at the lowest cost to the company, leaves the executive in a posture of aggressive contentment. Content not to seek other opportunities, but aggressive in the desire to earn the incentive portions of the total compensation package.

This chapter provides information on how companies establish internally equitable and externally competitive base salaries.

### Q. 3:1   How is an executive's base salary set?

Base salary is the amount of fixed cash compensation that is paid to an executive on a periodic basis that represents income that is not at risk. The Board of Directors typically sets the base salary of the Chief Executive Officer using market data obtained by the Board and there is a growing tendency, because of Board liability concerns, to use outside consultants to provide competitive compensation data from several independent sources. The company's compensation specialist is frequently used to collect all appropriate competitive practices information.

The other executive salaries are normally established by the Chief Executive Officer (CEO) who may or may not present this information for approval to the Board of Directors. The CEO receives both market data and either formally or informally reviews the executive's performance.

The Board of Directors and/or the Compensation Committee of the Board have a more formal obligation and interest in approving long-term plans that involve company stock (see Chapter 5).

### Q. 3:2   How do companies decide on salaries or salary ranges for executives?

Two approaches are typically used to peg the value of an executive position. Internal equity is determined by some form of job evaluation process and attempts, without any external reference, to determine which executive positions have more value to the corporation. External equity is determined by some method of data collection to establish what similar companies are paying for similar positions. The process of establishing external equity is referred to as market pricing. These two approaches, which are generally used in combination with each other, often give conflicting rankings of positions and therefore act as "checks" on each other. Using either formal statistical techniques or a more subjective management decision process, a dollar value range is typically assigned to each executive position. Typically, clusters of similarly valued positions are assigned to one salary range.

It is important to note, however, that in some industries base salary may be set at significantly lower levels than indicated by either the internal or external equity approach (see Q. 3:10). Where this is the case, bonuses are often used to compensate for the variance (see Chapters 4 and 5).

### Q. 3:3   What is job evaluation?

Job evaluation is the process that establishes the company's internal relative worth of a position by measuring a position's job duties against a predetermined yardstick. Job evaluation measures job worth in an internal sense rather than in an economic or social one.

A company establishes the economic worth of a position by looking outside the organization to see what the market is paying for a position while social worth is a function of the external perception of the importance of the contributions of a specific person or occupation. The internal concept of job worth involves the scope of responsibility or difficulty of assignments. Market worth, social worth and internal value are not identical and may not necessarily correlate.

This lack of correlation is one of the difficulties of job evaluation. As a result, there are hundreds of different methods of job evaluation, and all of them measure job responsibilities against a different pre-established yardstick. They differ in (1) Whether they measure the whole job or elements of the job and (2) How they assign values to the steps on the yardstick.

The four basic approaches to job evaluation are the:

- ranking system;
- classification system;
- point evaluation, and
- Factor comparison system.

# Job Evaluation Methodology for Executives

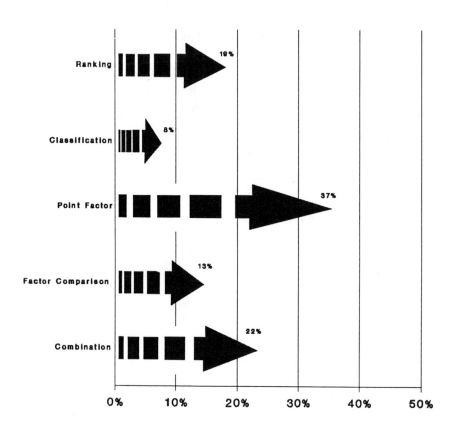

Source: Miller Mason & Dickenson, 1991

### Q. 3:4 How does the ranking system work?

In this approach the Chief Executive, usually with the help of the Chief Human Resource Executive, simply ranks one executive position against another. The CEO compares the two positions and decides which is more difficult or important. A third position is compared to the first two and so on until all jobs have been ranked. The advantage and disadvantage of this approach is the simplicity.

### Q. 3:5 How does a classification system work?

In a classification system each job is measured against a predetermined scale whose various categories define the overall value of the positions. The CEO typically compares each job against the scale and assigns each executive position into the grade that best describes the position.

### Q. 3:6 How does the point factor approach work?

The point factor system, which is the most widely used approach measures a position against a series of factors (e.g., administrative responsibility, technical expertise, financial impact) with each factor having a scale of points. A company can choose the factors it values and assign points on a scale based on how it relatively values those factors. Many companies use plans developed by companies that have predetermined factors and factor values.

### Q. 3:7 How does factor comparison work?

The factor comparison job evaluation approach ranks positions based on selected factors, without definitions or values for the various degrees. The CEO would analyze and rank all positions in terms of one factor then all positions in terms of the second factor. Only after all positions are evaluated are the points assigned to the position under each factor. The points are added to get the positions' overall relative value.

## Q. 3:7   What is market pricing?

Market pricing is the process by which a company identifies how comparable executive positions are paid in comparable organizations. In order to position executive base salaries relative to the market, they have to be "priced." Pricing executive positions is a critical activity. It is essential to establish a relationship between the base salaries of a company's executives with how other companies pay.

It is important to remember that the purpose of market pricing is to posture executives to the marketplace in a manner predetermined by a compensation philosophy. Because it is impossible to survey every company, a company needs to clearly define what market they want or need to be competitive with. Obviously, the more relevant the companies are the better the data obtained. Determining from which companies new executives are being recruited and to which companies executives are leaving, helps establish the competitive marketplace.

There are hundreds of surveys available to use in market pricing positions. Most organizations conduct customized surveys among competitor companies to establish a market for executive positions.

It is important to note that a company's compensation philosophy may not require base salary to directly reflect market pricing figures. Where base salary falls below those of other executives in the marketplace, bonus programs are often utilized to compensate for the variance (see Chapters 4 and 5).

## Q. 3:9   How do most companies position their executives' base salaries?

Most companies do not like to be perceived as "just average" in how they compensate their executives. In fact, surveys of compensation practices show that a significant number of companies try to pay at the 75th percentile. This compensation philosophy creates two significant problems. One obvious problem is that many companies are paying more than is necessary. The second problem is less obvious; if more than half the companies are trying to pay at the 75th percentile by comparing salaries reported in salary surveys then these companies are always chasing an ever increasing target. As every company increases their executive salaries to move them up to the 75th percentile, that percentile also increases. Consider a salary survey of five companies that reported the following salaries for CEO:

| Company | Base Salary |
|---------|-------------|
| A | $180,000 |
| B | $150,000 |
| C | $250,000 |
| D | $200,000 |
| E | $220,000 |

The average base salary is $200,000. Assume that the companies that pay below the average raise their CEO's salary to the average salary of $200,000, while the other companies give their CEO a 10 percent salary adjustment. Next year's average CEO salary will be $227,400. Not only will company A and B still be below the average but company D also falls below the new average. Chasing survey averages has built-in salary inflation.

# Job Evaluation Methodology
# for Executives

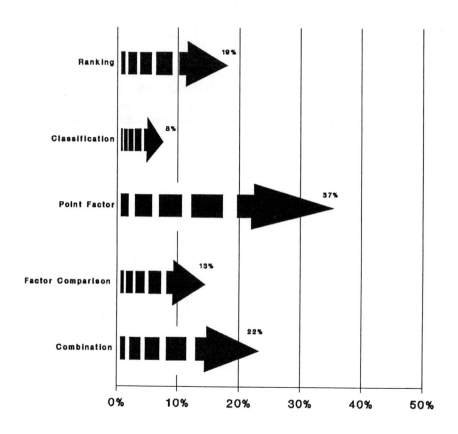

Source: Miller Mason & Dickenson, 1991

### Q. 3:10 Are there reasons for paying base salaries above or below the competitive average?

Yes. A base salary that is 10 percent above or below the competitive base salary as reported in a salary survey is probably a competitive posture. The best survey data is accurate at plus or minus 5 percent and most survey data is accurate at only the plus or minus ten percent level. In other words, being ten percent above or below the competitive level is being at the competitive level.

A company may need to pay a high base salary if there are no annual incentive or long-term incentive plans. If a company has other factors that make it unattractive as an employer, it may have to pay a premium base salary. For example, if the company is experiencing financial difficulties or if the company is in a geographically isolated area, it may have to pay a premium to attract executives. Frequently, a company in a slow or no growth environment may have to pay a premium to compensate for limited career promotion opportunities.

Most companies that pay seemingly low base salaries fall into several distinct categories. There are companies that are so specialized that their salaries can be low because executives cannot easily leave for another industry group. Health care has traditionally been such an industry. Another set of low paying companies are those companies whose financial situation is such that they simply cannot afford to pay competitive salaries. This underpayment posture is difficult to maintain in the long run and can have adverse impact on the tenure and quality of the executives involved. It becomes difficult to recruit or retain quality executives, if base salaries are not competitive although many companies compensate for low base salary by implementing bonus programs (see Chapters 4 and 5). The other extreme of low base paying companies are the high growth companies that can offer low base salaries in exchange for substantial long-term compensation and career movement opportunities. In high growth companies promotions and promotional salary adjustment can compensate for lower competitive salaries.

# Chapter 4

# Annual Incentives

The vast majority of companies provide annual incentive opportunities to their executive management team. While base salary remains the largest fixed element of an executive compensation package, the value of the annual incentives to the total package is growing. Companies use annual incentives to reward executives when the company and/or individual performance meets company expectations.

Two issues predominate any discussion on annual incentives. First, to what degree should executive, business unit or company performance impact an annual incentive payout? Second, what performance measures should be used to evaluate individual executives, business units and/or company performance?

This chapter provides a comprehensive overview of annual incentive plans and addresses why companies use annual incentives, in what circumstances they work best and the strengths and weaknesses of frequently used plans.

### Q. 4:1  How is short-term or annual incentive defined?

Annual incentive is a term that is frequently used interchangeably with short-term incentive. Short-term or annual incentive is usually defined as an incentive paid for performance over no more than one year. Usually these programs pay out the earned amount in cash (though some companies do pay all or part in stock). Short-term incentive plans can be formal or informal. If they are informal there may be no written plan and no predetermined funding method or participant allocation rules. Some companies prefer not to establish a formal annual incentive plan and instead simply have a policy of paying out bonuses annually that are based on the company's performance, without any predetermined funding method or participant allocation rules. This allows a company, within the context of overall firm performance, to provide incentives and rewards to executives based on their own individual performance. The informal method is most often recommended for small companies where the cost of creating a formal program is not justified, although an informal plan is appropriate for any company that feels that flexibility is necessary to retain the executives it wants most to retain by increasing their proportionate reward.

Most short-term incentive plans are designed to produce a payout for an executive that is either a specified percentage of base salary, or a percentage of a total target amount to be paid if company objectives are met.

A typical annual incentive plan would provide the following incentive opportunities:

| | |
|---|---|
| CEO | 40-60 percent |
| VP | 25-35 percent |
| Others | 20 percent |

The highest percentage potential is given to the highest ranking executive since it is assumed that he or she has the most responsibility for ensuring that the company achieves its annual objectives.

The payment for short-term incentive is usually made at the close of the plan cycle. A typical short-term cycle is either the calendar year or the company's fiscal year. However, voluntary or mandatory deferral is occasionally used for all or part of the earned amount. With the current low income tax rates and the belief that tax rates will rise in the future, few executives participate in voluntary deferral programs.

## Q. 4:2   How prevalent are annual incentive plans?

The vast majority of companies have an annual incentive plan. Surveys usually report that approximately 95 percent of companies have an annual incentive plan. Those few companies that do not have incentive plans believe that base salary (and performance based salary adjustments) can effectively distinguish between levels of performance. Compensation surveys show that while base salaries are somewhat higher in non-bonus companies, the additional money does not compensate for the lack of an incentive opportunity.

### Q. 4:3  What is the tax impact of annual incentive plans on the executive?

For a cash-basis company, annual cash incentive payments are deductible as and when the payments are actually made to the employee. For an accrual-basis company, amounts paid in cash to employees are deductible as and when the obligation to make the payments accrues, that is, when the liability for payment is fixed and definite and not subject to indeterminable future events. An exception to this rule is made for accrual-basis companies that have annual incentive plans based on performance that can only be determined after the end of their fiscal year. In this case, if the incentive plan uses a specific formula for payments, the accrual-basis company may be able to deduct amounts paid in respect of those bonuses even though it actually makes the payments up to two and one-half months after the end of the year. This is an additional factor for a company to consider in determining whether its annual plan should be formal or informal.

From the executive's point of view, he or she will, in all likelihood, recognize income in the year in which the payment is received, even if the company is able to deduct the payment in a different year. However, an accrual-basis individual will recognize income in the year in which it accrues.

Of course, the usual tax rules apply. Specifically, compensation must be reasonable and cannot be a disguised distribution of profits. However, an annual bonus may be deductible as a result of its contingent nature even where it would be considered unreasonable if it were paid in the form of salary because the executive is risking part of his or her compensation based on the company's performance. Because of this risk, he or she is entitled to a greater reward based on that performance.

Special consideration must be given when using informal plans because bonuses are generally determined when the company's performance and profits are known and there is, therefore, more of a risk that they may be deemed to constitute a distribution of earnings.

### Q. 4:4   What is the accounting treatment for annual incentive plans?

Like salaries, cash incentive payments are typically accrued as expenses for the accounting periods in which related services are performed. Any accrued but unpaid incentive payments are shown as liabilities on the balance sheet.

### Q. 4:5   What is the rationale for having an annual incentive plan?

Most companies believe that a primary reason for having an annual incentive plan is to motivate executives to achieve annual company operating goals. A second reason for incentive pay, especially for smaller revenue sized companies, is that these plans make a part of the executive payroll a variable cost. In highly capital intensive companies the total cost of bonus is an insignificant amount of after tax profits. However, in small, highly people intensive businesses, these payments can be a significant part of after tax profits.

Another rationale for having annual incentive plans is that if executives can make decisions and judgments that affect company results for the year, then it makes sense for these executives to have a significant part of their current earnings dependent upon the achievement of these results.

A final, but important reason for having an annual incentive plan is to offer competitive compensation programs that in turn can attract and retain executives. With over 95 percent of companies offering executives annual incentives, a company would be at a recruiting disadvantage without a program. However, it is interesting to note that while executives in the recruitment situation seem to be concerned about the existence of a program, they rarely question how much the plan paid out in the past, perhaps because of the expectation that such plans will pay off in the future.

**Planning Tip:** Incentive programs need "sunsets". Most programs need revision or modification over time. Incentive plans, over time, lose their effectiveness. Plans should have a three-year expiration cycle. Every three years a review of participation, performance goals and payout should be made. Without a "sunset" provision, plans tend to continue without revision.

## Q. 4:6  How is the typical annual incentive payment made?

Typically, short-term or annual incentive plans pay their awards in cash because plans that pay out their rewards in stock are generally conceptualized as long-term incentive plans. However, a number of companies are beginning to pay out at least a portion of their annual bonuses in the form of company stock, usually restricted stock, and this possibility should be considered as you read this chapter.

## Q. 4:7  What are the key issues in the design of an annual incentive program?

There are many important issues to address in the design and/or review of an annual incentive program. Some of these issues are:

1.  What is the appropriate incentive plan payout? What should the payout be if the business objectives are achieved?

2.  What is the appropriate measure of business performance? What measure (i.e., sales growth, return of equity, earnings per share) should be used to evaluate performance?

3.  What is the appropriate level of performance on the established measure to warrant payment of the standard incentive payout? If sales growth is chosen, what percentage of sales growth generates the normal payout?

4.  What is the appropriate leverage? How much should an executive receive for exceeding the objective; and how much should the executive be penalized for not achieving the objective?

5.  What is the appropriate threshold level, both in amount and type?

6.  What is the appropriate mix of company performance, individual performance and/or business unit performance?

Another issue is whether there should be a maximum payout in an executive incentive plan. Most plans do put caps on either how much an individual can earn or how big the group incentive pool can be and these caps are usually set at 1.5 or 2 times the standard bonus.

### Q. 4:8 What are the basic plan designs for annual incentive plans?

The basic plan designs for annual incentive plans are:

- Percent-of-profits;
- Growth or improvement plans;
- Target performance plans;
- Peer company comparisons plans; and
- Matrix plans.

Most annual incentive plans incorporate threshold levels, which are levels below which no incentive plan payouts are made. In some cases the threshold level is referred to as the deductible because the first profit amounts are "deducted" from any plan payout considerations. A threshold level can be established on the chosen incentive plan goal or can be established using a separate criterion.

Some typical threshold levels used in incentive plans are:

- **Competitor level:** No incentive payout will be made on a given performance measure unless the company outperforms a specified percentage performance measure of the competitor companies.
- **Dividend payments:** No incentive plan payout will be made unless there are sufficient profits to cover the desired dividend.
- **Alternate investment:** No incentive plan payout will be made unless the return equals the available return from the specified source (i.e., short-term money market or certificate of deposit.
- **Interest rate:** No incentive plan payout will be made unless the return is at least at the prime interest rate level.
- **Past performance:** No incentive payments are made unless the return exceeds by a specified percentage the average of the last three years.

The threshold measure and level vary greatly, but they should always reflect the environment in which the company is operating and the business strategy of the company. Finally, the threshold should not be set so low that the incentive payout is guaranteed, nor should it be set so high as to be unattainable. (For a discussion of the various types of performance standards see Q. 4:24–Q. 4:40.)

In all of these plans, a company must determine whether the payout should be based on group or individual performance. See Q. 4:35–Q. 4:40 for a discussion of the differences between the pool method and the participant method.

### Q. 4:9   How does a percentage-of-profits plan operate?

Under a percentage-of-profits plan the company pays a predetermined percentage of company or division profits as a cash bonus to selected participants. There usually is not a performance threshold level such as an earnings target or return on stockholder equity.

**Example:** Company A has a percentage-of-profits plan incentive plan. It allocates 7 percent of after-tax profits to a pool to be shared among its twelve executives. This amount is allocated among executives in the following manner.

| | |
|---|---|
| CEO | 25 percent |
| COO | 13 percent |
| CFO | 8 percent |
| Other 9 executives | 6 percent |

At the end of the 1992 fiscal year, sales were $36 million. After-tax profits were $5 million yielding a 13.9 percent profit margin. The pool would be $350,000 ($5M × 7 percent). The incentive would be distributed as follows:

| | |
|---|---|
| CEO | 0.25 × $350,000 = $87,500 |
| COO | 0.13 × $350,000 = $45,500 |
| CFO | 0.08 × $350,000 = $28,000 |
| Other 9 executives | 0.06 × $350,000 = $21,000 |

### Q. 4:10   What are the advantages of a percent-of-profits plan?

There are several distinct advantages to a percent-of-profits plan. They include:

- The plan is easily understood by participants;
- No incentive plan payouts occur unless the company or division is profitable; and

- Incentive plan payouts increase in direct proportion to profits.

### Q. 4:11   What are the disadvantages of a percent of profits plan?

The primary disadvantage of this type of plan is that incentive plan payout are open-ended, possibly resulting in large windfalls.

**Example:** The facts are the same as in the example at Question 4:9 except that over time, the plan was not changed, but through acquisition and growth, the company became a $120 million revenue company. Assume that the profit margin had declined to 10 percent from 13.9 percent, a 29 percent decline, to yield $12 million in after-tax profits. The bonus pool would have increased to $840,000 (7 percent × $12M). The incentive payments would have increased to:

| | |
|---|---|
| CEO | 0.25 × $840,000 = $210,000 |
| COO | 0.13 × $840,000 = $109,200 |
| CFO | 0.08 × $840,000 = $ 67,200 |
| Other 9 executives | 0.06 × $840,000 = $ 50,400 |

Bonuses would have increased more than 100 percent, but operating performance would have declined.

The other disadvantage of a percent-of-profit plan is that the amount of capital needed to produce the profit does not play a role in measuring performance.

### Q. 4:12   How does a growth or improvement plan operate?

Typically a company selects one or more performance factors (net earnings, earnings per share or sales growth are commonly used; see Q. 4:26). The incentive pool is created based upon improvement over prior year's results. The average of several prior years may be utilized to minimize year-to-year variations. A percentage of increased profits, revenues or sales growth is typically used to create the pool.

**Example:** Company C has a growth or improvement plan in which its executives share as follows:

| | |
|---|---|
| CEO | 25 percent |
| COO | 13 percent |
| CFO | 8 percent |
| Other 9 executives | 6 percent |

Company C's after-tax profits during the prior three years averaged $5 million and Company C decides to allocate to the pool 50 percent of its after-tax profits in excess of $5.5 million, an increase of 10% over the prior three-year averages. If profit is below $5.5 million, the incentive plan will not provide a payout. If Company C's after-tax return hits $6.2 million, the pool, therefore, is $350,000 (0.7 million × 0.50). The distribution would be:

| | |
|---|---|
| CEO | 0.25 × $350,000 = $87,500 |
| COO | 0.13 × $350,000 = $45,500 |
| CFO | 0.08 × $350,000 = $28,000 |
| Other 9 executives | 0.06 × $350,000 = $21,000 |

### Q. 4:13 What are the advantages of a growth or improvement plan?

The distinct strength of this type of plan is the process of identifying one or more performance criteria. The identification of the appropriate criteria results in executives perceiving the plan as more objective. The growth plan also focuses on improvement rather than fixed performance levels. This plan is ideal, if a company believes that base salary compensates an executive for managing the firm and incentive plans reward for additional effort and improvement in performance. Since the plan focuses on improvement there is no need for accurate forecasting of business conditions and performance targets.

### Q. 4:14 What are the disadvantages of a growth or improvement plan?

There are several drawbacks to these types of plans. Improvement over past results are not always feasible in declining areas or mature industries.

**Example:** The facts are the same as in the example at Question 4:12 except that the economy fell into a major recession, and Company C saw its product demand evaporate. However, through cost cutting and new products, Company C somehow achieved a $5 million after-tax profit, even when their competitors were losing money. Under the growth or improvement plan, none of the executives would have received a bonus.

Conversely, in other areas or industries, improvement over past results may not indicate good management performance. For example, a company's ten percent growth rate may indicate poor performance in a high growth industry where demand is increasing at a 25 percent rate. In addition, improvement over a period of poor performance may still be unacceptable performance. In periods of cyclical or fluctuating profits, executives can be rewarded for the same improvement over and over.

### Q. 4:15  How does the target performance plan work?

Under the target performance plan, the company establishes "target," "minimum," and "optimistic" performance levels based on percentage increases over the prior year's results or over other measures (see Q. 4:30) on a company-wide and/or division-wide basis to create an incentive pool. The company has the choice of setting aside either a fixed percentage of executive salaries or a fixed percentage of after-tax profits in the incentive pool for awards when the minimum is reached and it also has the choice of which results to measure for purposes of the plan (see Q. 2:24). The pool increases based upon results until the maximum is reached. This approach is widely used and is easily adopted to individual business units.

**Example:** Company D has a target performance plan. The following performance matrix is established to determine incentive payments (as a percentage of the executive base salary):

**After-tax Returns**

| Position | Minimum 10.0% | Target 14.0% | Optimistic 18.0% |
|---|---|---|---|
| CEO | 25% | 50% | 60% |
| COO | 20% | 40% | 48% |
| CFO | 15% | 30% | 36% |
| Others | 12.5% | 25% | 30% |

If the target of a 14 percent increase in the chosen performance factor is achieved, the payout would be:

| Title | Base Salary | Percentage | Payout |
|-------|-------------|------------|--------|
| CEO | $200,000 | 50% | $100,000 |
| COO | 160,000 | 40% | 64,000 |
| CFO | 125,000 | 30% | 37,500 |
| Executive 1 | 110,000 | 25% | 27,500 |
| Executive 2 | 88,000 | 25% | 22,000 |
| Executive 3 | 88,000 | 25% | 22,000 |
| Executive 4 | 76,000 | 25% | 19,000 |
| Executive 5 | 75,000 | 25% | 18,750 |
| Executive 6 | 70,000 | 25% | 17,500 |
| Executive 7 | 68,000 | 25% | 17,000 |
| Executive 8 | 68,000 | 25% | 17,000 |
| Executive 9 | 65,000 | 25% | 16,250 |

If the performance level fell between the defined targets, for example, 12 percent, the incentive payments could be extrapolated or only the lower target amount paid out.

### Q. 4:16  What are the advantages of a target performance plan?

A target performance plan clearly establishes the criteria for generating the incentive pool based on the business plan. If the pool is based upon participant salaries, it automatically increases in relation to new participants. Shareholder interest can be protected by the way the minimum performance level is established and how the maximum level is capped. The shareholder can be assured of a return before bonuses are paid and maximum payout are known.

### Q. 4:17  What are the disadvantages of a target performance plan?

The primary disadvantage of this type of plan is that it is time-consuming to establish. Targets must be established each year which requires accurate forecasting of company results, external business conditions and competition to establish accurate target, minimum and optimistic objective levels.

## Q. 4:18    How does a peer company performance plan operate?

The company selects one or more financial measures and a group of competitor companies to be compared against. An incentive pool is created based upon performance relative to the peer group results with an increasing pool for increasing relative performance. A percentage of participant salaries, predetermined amounts or a percentage of profits are tied to the various performance levels to create the pool.

**Example:** Hospital A has identified bed occupancy (the percentage of hospital beds that are utilized over the year) as the prime objective next year. During the current year, bed occupancy was 76 percent. In the geographic area that Hospital A competes in the average bed occupancy is 78 percent. The following matrix determines the payout as a percentage of executive base salary:

### Bed Occupancy

| Position | Average | 2% Above Average | 4% Above Average |
|----------|---------|------------------|------------------|
| CEO | 40% | 48% | 52% |
| CFO | 30% | 36% | 39% |
| COO | 20% | 22% | 26% |
| Others | 15% | 16.5% | 19.5% |

If, during the next year, bed occupancy for the region was again at 78 percent and Hospital A improved its bed occupancy to 78 percent, the incentive payout would be from the first column average. But, assume that average bed occupancy for the region dropped to 60 percent and Hospital A's bed occupancy dropped to 70 percent. Despite this drop in bed occupancy, Hospital A would pay the highest level of bonus (the third column because Hospital A's bed occupancy was more than 4 percent above the average.

### Q. 4:19 What are the advantages of a peer company performance plan?

This type of plan insulates the company's performance from uncontrollable market conditions since these conditions should, in theory, affect all companies to the same degree. The need for accurate forecasting is unnecessary. It reinforces the shareholder interest. If any investor has chosen to invest in a given industry, that investor wants to invest in the company that outperforms the other companies in that industry, that is the company that has the best returns in the industry.

### Q. 4:20 What are the disadvantages of a peer comparison plan?

The greatest difficulty with this plan is related to comparison factors. Data may not be available for all competitors. These plans are most common among companies in industries which are easily defined and produce uniform and easily available financial data. Banking and hospitals are two industries that meet these criteria and frequently use peer comparison plans.

### Q. 4:21 What are the key features of a matrix plan?

With a matrix plan, the company establishes a two or three dimensional performance matrix for each level of executive covered, incorporating various performance measures (see Q. 2:24) and indicating the percentage of salary or after-tax profit payable at various performance levels. Frequently, these plans use two or more design features or utilize two or more performance measures. Though primarily used in annual incentive plans, this plan design approach is also utilized in long-term incentive plans, such as performance unit plans (see Chapter 7).

**Example:** Company E has a matrix incentive plan. Their performance measures are sales growth and Return on Investment. The payout matrix for the CEO position is:

If the sales growth target of 14 percent and the Return on Investment (ROI) target of 8 percent is achieved, the CEO would receive a 50-percent-of-base-salary annual incentive. Performance below 6 percent sales growth or below 6 percent ROI, would result in no incentive payment. The incentive payment is capped at 90 percent of base salary so that performance above 12 percent of ROI or 18 percent sales growth would still provide a 90 percent incentive payment. Performance between the established points (for example, ROI of 6.5 and sales growth of 8 percent) could be extrapolated or earn the lower payout amount. Similarly, if the two payout measures come in under different payout matrices, the payout could also be extrapolated or earn the lower amount.

## Q. 4:22   What are the advantages of a matrix plan?

A matrix plan focuses an executive on two or three significant performance measures. This approach also facilitates nonlinear weighing of performance levels. For example, an eight percent earnings growth may earn an incentive payment only if it is at the 75th percentile of an industry group.

## Q. 4:23   What are the disadvantages of a matrix plan?

A matrix plan requires accurate forecasting and target setting. The more targets involved, the more likely that an inappropriate target or performance measure is chosen.

## Q. 4:24   How can you determine whether your performance standards are appropriate?

If performance standards are too high and are never or rarely achieved resulting in no incentive payments executives will perceive these standards as being unattainable and the incentives actually will become disincentives. If performance standards are too low and are always achieved, the incentive plan becomes part of the salary program. An easy way to spot this is to measure the Parsons ratio of the incentive payments (see Q. 4:25).

A rule of thumb in establishing performance standards is that in a ten year period there would be one or two years in which there are no incentive payments and there would be one or two years where incentive payments would be at the maximum level.

While incentive payments do fluctuate in companies, it is becoming increasingly rare for an executive who is a participant in an annual incentive plan to receive no incentive payment. If an executive is eligible for an incentive payment of up to 40 percent of base salary, but over a prolonged time span is always earning between 20 to 40 percent and never earns less than 20 percent, it makes more sense to build that 20 percent into the base salary and offer the remainder as a true variable incentive payment.

### Q. 4:25    What is the Parsons ratio?

The Parsons ratio is the earned annual incentive payments, typically over a five year period, as a percentage of the total possible incentive payments over a five year period. A high Parsons ratio would indicate that most executives annually earn the maximum amount allowable under the incentive plan. This could indicate performance objectives that are too easily achieved. Conversely, a low ratio would indicate a company that is performing poorly or whose performance objectives may be too demanding and, therefore, not achievable. In practice there is no standard or "correct" Parsons ratio because such a ratio will necessarily vary from company to company.

### Q. 4:26    What are commonly used company performance measures for annual incentive plans?

Most companies rely on quantitative financial measures for their annual incentive plans. Target earnings are frequently used even though that performance measure has the limitation that it does not reflect the effects of inflation on the company's performance. Other companies use financial ratios such as return on assets and return on equity. The shortcoming of these ratios is that they reflect an accounting value of the investment base, rather than current cost levels. These shortcomings can be overcome by restating accounting measures to reflect replacement costs and measuring returns using cash flow. Size of company and maturity of the company also impact the types of measures used.

Most companies use more than one performance measure although each additional performance standard increases the complexity and decreases the understanding of the plan. Companies cannot and should not attempt to direct all elements of the management function through the use of an annual incentive plan. However, companies often try to include all management performance measures in the annual incentive plan, which is an error because certain types of management performance do not correlate to an annual timetable.

The most frequently used performance measures are:

- Target earnings;
- Target sales;
- Increases in profits or earnings per share growth;
- Increases in sales;
- Profit margin;
- Return on capital;
- Return on assets; and
- Return on equity.

Small companies in high growth cycles frequently use target sales as a measure.

### Q. 4:27   What is earnings per share and how is it calculated?

Earnings per share (EPS) is a frequently encountered measure of profitability. This ratio is computed by dividing net income attributable to common stock by the average number of common shares outstanding. Earnings per share has been criticized as a measure of profitability because it does not consider the amount of assets or capital required to generate that level of earnings. Two firms with the same earnings per share will not be equally profitable if one of the firms requires twice the amount of assets or capital to generate those earnings than does the other firm. Despite this limitation EPS is a commonly accepted management performance criteria.

### Q. 4:28   What is return on assets and how is it calculated?

Return on assets is an effective way to assess management's performance in using assets to generate earnings. This measure is often called the return on investment and is calculated by adding net income, interest expense net of income tax savings and minority interest in earnings. This amount is divided by average total assets.

Because the earnings rate during the year is being computed, the measure of investment should reflect the average amount of assets during the year.

### Q. 4:29   How is return on equity calculated?

The shareholder is probably more interested in the rate of return on common shareholder's equity than the rate of return on assets. To compute the amount of earnings attributable to common stock, dividends on preferred stock must be deducted from net income. The capital provided during the period by common shareholders can be determined by averaging the aggregate par value of common stock, capital contributed in excess of par value on common stock and retained earnings at the beginning and end of the period.

### Q. 4:30   What are the basic methods of performance comparison in annual incentive plans and how are they established?

Once the performance measures have been chosen, the most critical aspect in the design of an annual incentive plan is the setting of performance standards. The specifics of setting performance standards vary a great deal between types of companies and within industries but the general guidelines set forth in Questions 4:24 and 4:42 regarding the size of the actual payout do apply.

Generally, performance targets should expect improvement over time. How much improvement is a function of many things. There are four typical ways to establish performance targets. They are:

1. The "look around" method;
2. The "look behind" method;
3. The "look forward" method; and
4. The "don't look" approach.

As you will note, many of these measures equate directly to the plans that are based on them.

### Q. 4:31   How does the "look-ahead" approach in performance comparison work?

In a "look-ahead" plan, actual performance is measured against targets that are established each year based on business plans. This approach is the most prevalent plan design in annual plans. Its obvious advantage is that it focuses on the annual business plan.

### Q. 4:32   How does the "look-around" approach in performance comparison work?

In the peer group or "look-around" approach, actual performance is measured against performance of a group of competitor companies. This approach focuses on relative performance against competitor firms. It is only appropriate where timely and accurate competitor data is available. It is frequently used in banks, saving and loans and utilities. The basic assumption in this plan is that outside forces will have had a similar effect on both the company's and comparison group's performance. A company that has performed better than the comparison group is assumed to have demonstrated above average performance.

### Q. 4:33   How does the "look-back" approach in performance comparison work?

The improvement or "look-back" plan compares a company's performance with prior company performance. Look-back plans are most often established by young, growth oriented companies, where accurate forecasting is difficult. One weakness of this plan design is that improvement over prior performance may not be an indicator of good performance.

### Q. 4:34   How does the fixed or "don't-look" approach in performance comparison work?

A fixed or "don't-look" plan allocates a fixed percentage of income to be used to fund a bonus pool. This fairly common approach results in a bonus pool funding without reference to a business plan or economic conditions. The drawback to this approach is that these fixed percentages tend to stay in place for many years thereby not being responsive to economic conditions and competitive practice.

### Q. 4:35 How does a company decide whether the incentive programs should be based on group or individual performance?

A company must consider whether it is possible and/or practical to establish performance targets for an individual executive's performance. While conceptually attractive, setting individual targets is time consuming. Most companies base incentives initially on group performance (corporate, divisional or departmental) and use individual targets as an adjustment to the amount generated by the group performance. This approach balances the organization's need for team-work while recognizing the individual's contribution. Generally, this balancing is accomplished by making a portion of the incentive payout earned by formula with the remainder based on the executive's supervisor evaluation of individual performance. This approach is compatible with the most prevalent types of plan design.

### Q. 4:36 How does the pool method operate?

The pool method is a popular method of determining an incentive payout. An overall incentive "pool" is calculated for all participants or a group of participants and each individual's award is then determined as a share of the pool.

### Q. 4:37 Are there advantages of the pool method?

Yes. The primary advantage is that it limits aggregate payout and costs regardless of the number of participants or level of performance.

### Q. 4:38 Are there disadvantages of the pool method?

Yes, there are two basic disadvantages to the pool method. The disadvantages to this approach are:

1. Superior performance by one person can be rewarded only by reducing the share of the pool of other participants; and

2. New participants dilute the available incentive payment of existing participants.

### Q. 4:39  How does the participant method work?

Each participant has an incentive opportunity that is not affected by the performance of other participants (although the individual's own award may be adjusted based on his or her performance). The total payout is merely the sum of individual participants awards.

### Q. 4:40  Are there advantages to the participant method?

Yes. The participant method makes it much easier to communicate the incentive opportunity to participants. In addition, it is a flexible design that responds to changing numbers of participants and individual responsibilities of participants.

### Q. 4:41  How is eligibility in annual incentive plans typically determined?

Participation should be limited to those individuals who can substantially affect the performance measures used in the incentive plan. In practice, competitive practices are often the deciding factors. If a position would be incentive eligible in other companies, that position is typically made eligible for the incentive plan.

As a rule of thumb, 2 percent of the executives participate in annual incentive plans. There is however, great variance in this figure. Highly capital intensive industries have fewer participants. Highly people intensive firms have a larger percentage of participants.

# Performance Thresholds
## General Industry

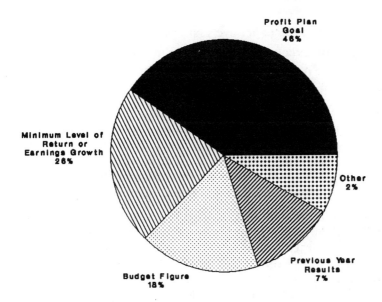

Profit Plan
Goal
46%

Minimum Level of
Return or
Earnings Growth
26%

Other
2%

Budget Figure
18%

Previous Year
Results
7%

Source:  Sibson 1991 Annual Report

**Planning Tip:** Two considerations should be used in determining eligibility for annual incentive plans. An incentive plan should include those executives whose performance will significantly impact the results of the company or a business unit. In addition, an incentive plan should include those positions which in other organizations would be included in an annual incentive plan.

### Q. 4:42 What are typical annual incentive amounts paid to executives?

Four factors determine the amount of incentive pay an executive receives:

1. The amount of the executive's base salary;
2. The level the executive occupies within the organization;
3. The industry the executive works in; and
4. The individual performance of the company.

*Base Salary:* Typically, the higher the base salary the larger the incentive opportunity (both as a percentage of base and, of course, the amount). For example, a Chief Executive Officer earning $200,000 will probably be eligible for a larger incentive payment than an CEO earning $100,000. This is partly explained by the fact that base salaries are significantly affected by size of corporation.

*Organizational Level:* The CEO normally is eligible for the largest incentive opportunity. Typically, his direct reports are eligible for 70 to 80 percent of the CEO bonus (expressed as a percentage). For example, if the CEO's bonus target is 50 percent of base salary his direct reports will be eligible for between 35 to 40 percent of their base salary. The next reporting level typically is eligible to receive between 50 and 60 percent of the CEO's percentage.

*Industry:* Manufacturing and Banking tend to pay larger incentive amounts then do industries such as health care or insurance.

*Individual Company Performance:* One normally would assume that the better the company performance the larger the amount the executive would receive as incentive payments. In most cases this holds true when analyzing individual company plans and payout. When looking at one specific company, incentive payments will typically be larger in those years where performance was better. However, an analysis across many companies shows that poor performing companies on the average make better incentive payments than do companies performing at higher levels. This phenomenon holds true regardless of which performance criteria are used.

Because many companies establish annual incentive payment targets based on prior years' performance, poorly performing companies tend to establish lower performance targets. For example, a company that is losing money may see "breaking even" as excellent management performance, worthy of incentive payments. However, another company which historically has made a 20 percent return on investment may establish their targets at 22 percent return on investment. In the long run it will be easier for a poorly performing company to improve performance (break even and pay a bonus) than it will for a higher performing company to improve their performance.

### Q. 4:43  Do incentive plans have maximum or caps on incentive payments?

Most incentive plans do cap the potential payout opportunities so that managers would not benefit by events which are beyond the control of management. Many companies feel that performance that substantially exceeds budgeted targets is more a reflection of poor budgeting rather than excellent executive performance.

The arguments against capping incentive payout are twofold. The first is that if the goal is to tie performance to payout, then it follows that if performance exceeds all expectations then the incentive payment should exceed all expectations. Second, if the executive is at risk on the downside (i.e., he or she could receive nothing even if it is the result of bad budgeting) he/she should have the upside potential uncapped.

A cap on incentive plan payouts may be expressed as an absolute dollar limitation (either on contributions to the pool or on individual awards) or as a percentage or multiple of the projected maximum payout.

### Q. 4:44   Is shareholder approval required for annual incentive plans?

Shareholder approval is required for annual incentive plans only if the plan design or payment uses company stock. However, many companies do seek shareholder approval simply because they feel it is appropriate from a shareholder relations point of view.

# Chapter 5

# Long-Term Incentive Plan Overview

Long-term incentive programs, frequently referred to as capital accumulation plans, are offered to executives by a majority of companies. In fact, participation in these plans was traditionally used as the definition for who was considered an "executive." Three basic plan designs are utilized when implementing a long-term incentive plan. The first, purchase plans, require an executive to make an investment while the second, appreciation plans, grant the executive the right to receive the value of the appreciation in the employer's stock and the third, full-value plans, grant the executive the full value of the company stock plus any appreciation that may result over a period of years. This chapter provides an overview of the issues that impact how long-term plans are designed and administered. Chapter 6 deals specifically with purchase plans while Chapter 7 covers appreciation and full-value plans. Lastly, Chapter 8 deals with the effects of combining two different long-term plans.

## Q. 5:1 What are long-term incentive plans?

Long-term incentive plans or capital accumulation plans are long-term programs that give executives the opportunity to accumulate estate building capital when the value of the company's stock increases or when long-term company objectives are met. Since stock options are the most prevalent type of capital accumulation plan, many individuals use the term "stock options" interchangeably with the term "capital accumulation plans." Stock options are only one approach to capital accumulation and long-term incentives.

### Q. 5:2   What are the characteristics of long-term incentive plans?

Long-term incentive plans usually are structured with a three- to five-year time frame. However, to provide continuous incentives, many companies make annual grants that may subsequently result in annual payments. Long-term plans are generally stock-based or use increases in stock prices as the basis for payouts, because they are designed to create an interest in the executive that mirrors the interest of the company's shareholders. Payments are typically made in stock, cash or a combination and if the combination approach is used, sufficient cash is paid out or withheld to cover the executive's tax obligation for the stock and/or cash received.

### Q. 5:3   How is eligibility for participation in long-term plans determined?

Only those executives who can make decisions that affect a company's long-term results usually participate in long-term incentive plans and, when this criteria is used, the participation in long-term plans is usually limited to a handful of executives. However, survey information regarding Fortune 500 companies shows that the trend is for expanding the individuals who are eligible for long-term plans to middle managers so that the eligibility for long-term incentive opportunities now begins in the low-sixty-thousand-dollar salary levels.

Emerging and growth companies that may have cost and cash-flow problems tend to include larger numbers of executives in these programs to compensate for lower base salaries as well as to use long-term plans, with accompanying prospects of huge future payouts as a recruitment and retention tool.

Most companies use long-term plan participation as a motivator so that the executives selected for participation are given the message that they have been selected for membership in a special group.

### Q. 5:4   How prevalent are long-term incentive plans?

The majority of publicly-traded companies offer some form of long-term incentive for their executives.

### Q. 5:5   What is the rationale for having long-term incentive plans?

The prime reason most companies provide long-term incentive plans is that they believe that giving the executives an ownership potential or position will be an effective motivator. A second reason is that long-term incentive plans are a way to diffuse widespread criticism that management focuses on short-term results rather than the priorities of long-term growth and profitability. A third reason is a strictly financial one.

Furthermore, companies offer long-term incentive programs because they believe they are necessary to recruit and retain top-quality executives. This is probably the worst, yet most common rationale for instituting long-term incentive programs and is unfortunate, because such a "me-too" attitude can prevent organizations from developing programs that will best benefit their business.

### Q. 5:6   What are the criteria for distinguishing between different types of capital accumulation plans?

In reviewing the numerous alternatives, there are some basic questions that, if evaluated honestly, will help determine which type of plan design most effectively meets the employer's strategic compensation goals. The following checklist is designed to outline the questions that should be considered.

#### Capital Accumulation Characteristic Checklist

Evaluate the following key issues:
1. *Executive Investment.* Will the executive be required to make an investment or will he participate in the plan without an investment?
2. *Ownership.* Will the objective of the program be to create ownership of stock by the executive, or is the intent to reward the

executive for improvement in stock price or other financial measures?

3. *Company Impact.* What percentage of company shares should be set aside for the long-term incentive plan? How much dilution or direct charge to earnings is appropriate?

4. *Performance Factors.* What performance factor is indicative of long-term success? Is it stock price performance criteria, or is it some other measure, such as earnings-per-share, or return on investment?

5. *Accounting and Tax Impact.* What is the tax, accounting and financial impact on the company and/or the executive?

   A. The impact of the plan's tax treatment:
     —When will the taxable event occur for the executive and, as a result, entitle the company to a corresponding compensation deduction?

      • On grant;

      • Some other date prior to receiving payment; or

      • Upon sale and realization of cash?

     —How will the plan impact on the executive's tax situation?

      • Will the awards be subject to a potential alternative minimum tax (AMT) liability?

      • Will the awards be taxed at mostly ordinary income or capital gains rates?

   B. The impact of the plan on financial issues:
     —Is the payout chargeable as an expense against the company's income?

     —Must the payout be accrued as a liability on the company's books?

     —If so, when and in what amounts?

     —Is there an impact on capital accounts?

     —What is the earnings per share impact?

6. *Payout Levels.* What level of payout should the executive receive when long-term objectives are achieved? How much capital accumulation is appropriate and fair to the company, the shareholders and the executive?

7. *Grant Frequency.* How often should long-term plan grants and/or awards be made?

8. *Corporate and Legal Restrictions.* What corporate and legal restrictions impact on the company and/or the executive?

   A. The impact of federal and state securities law on the plan:
      — Do the interests or benefits provided by the program have to be registered under federal or state law?
      — Will a privately-held company become subject to rules pertaining to publicly-traded companies?

   B. The impact of the plan on general corporate operations:
      — Will the plan create a minority shareholder that, in the case of a privately-held company, could impact the management of the company?
      — Will the plan create a second class of stock, result in more than 35 shareholders, or otherwise terminate an S corporation election?

## Q. 5:6 What are the principal types of long-term incentive plans?

There are several variations on the long-term incentive plan although stock options and stock appreciation rights (SARs) are the most frequently utilized plan designs (although SARs have recently lost much of their appeal as a compensation device). Performance share and performance unit plans are also commonly used and restricted stock has recently had a resurgence in use. Most plans can be categorized into four basic plan designs.

The first category includes plans that will provide the executive with stock, provided that he or she makes an investment; these plans are the most common type of long-term incentive plan and are called purchase plans (see Chapter 6). The second category of plans includes plans that grant the executive the appreciation in the employer's stock over a certain period but not the value of the stock itself at the time of grant. These plans are aptly known as appreciation plans. The third category of plans includes plans that grant the executive not only any appreciation in the value of the stock over a specified period of time but also the value of the stock at time of grant. These plans are called full-value plans because the executive receives all of the benefits of the grant without having to actually make an investment. (Both appreciation and full-value plans are covered in detail in Chapter 7.) Finally, there are combination plans, which utilize two or more plan types. (Combination plans are discussed in detail at Chapter 8.)

### Q. 5:8  What is a long-term cash plan?

A long-term cash plan pays cash when long-term objectives are achieved. It is similar in design to short-term incentive plans, except that the performance cycle is typically three to five years. The typical long-term cash plan pays out less than the sum of the short-term incentive payments over the same period of time.

### Q. 5:9  Are there advantages of stock option plans as compared to long-term cash plans?

Yes. First and foremost, there is no out-of-pocket cost to the company. In addition, there is no accounting charge against the company's earnings, if the option is granted at full value, that is, the option exercise price is the then-market value of the shares of common stock covered by the option. And, if the option is a nonqualified option, the company receives a tax deduction upon exercise.

Stock options provide the executive potentially large capital accumulation opportunities. Possibly the most significant advantage may be the psychic benefits. Options identify an executive as part of a small, elite team of key players. They also tie one's rewards to what shareholders care most about—the price of the company stock.

### Q. 5:10  Are there disadvantages to using stock options as compared to long-term cash plans?

Yes. The "sale" of shares under a stock-option plan must be registered under the 1933 Act, generally on a Form S-8, while a long-term cash plan is free from any registration requirements. However, with the new revised S-8 rules the effective disadvantage is minimal.

### Q. 5:11   Under what circumstances is a long-term cash plan effective?

In privately-held companies, where ownership dilution is a concern, long-term cash plans are an alternative to stock-based plans. In addition, any companies whose stock is thinly traded and, therefore, have slow or erratic growth in stock price, can also benefit from a cash-based plan.

### Q. 5:12   What is the rationale behind using stock-based plans?

As a long-term incentive, the economic benefit to an executive of a stock-based plan can be duplicated through the use of a cash-based plan. However, it is much cheaper for the employer-company to use stock in compensating its executives than it is to pay them the cash value of that stock. Furthermore, the idea behind any compensation scheme is to motivate executives to do what is best for the company and its shareholders and there is no better way to accomplish this than by making sure that their interests are the same by tying the executive's compensation to the stock performance.

In addition, publicly-traded corporations like to use stock-based plans because this enables them to plan a large block of stock in "friendly" hands, which makes takeover attempts more difficult. Privately-held corporations can also benefit from using stock-based plans as a way of gradually transferring ownership or voting control.

### Q. 5:13   What are the general rules regarding taxation of capital accumulation plans?

To the extent that the executive is taxed on the benefit as ordinary income, the company receives a corresponding federal income tax deduction. Plans which defer the executive's recognition of income will also defer the date on which the company may claim a tax deduction.

### Q. 5:14  What are the basic accounting issues for capital accumulation plans?

The basic issue for accounting purposes is whether a given cost associated with a capital accumulation plan benefit will be expensed currently or whether it will be treated as a capital item that is expensed as the contribution costs are actually accrued. While certain plan benefits traditionally have been expensed, others that provide the same benefits in almost the same way are treated as a capital item and, as result, the basic accounting treatment for capital accumulation plans is somewhat contradictory and inconsistent.

Consider for example, that options granted at market value produce a benefit that is treated as a capital item and not expensed, however a similar benefit provided by a stock appreciation plan is treated as an expense. Both plans (stock option and stock appreciation rights) produce a similar benefit to the executive which is the appreciation of the stock price over a period of time. However the accounting treatment to the company differs substantially.

The Financial Accounting Standards Board (FASB) has been reviewing the accounting treatments for capital accumulation programs for several years. There is some agreement within FASB and the accounting profession that stock options should be treated as compensation items rather than capital items and should be expensed at the date of grant. However, there is much disagreement on the measure of the expense. Should the value of the benefit be the value at time of grant or the future value at the time of exercise or sale? The value at grant underestimates the benefit to the executive. The value in the future involves making assumptions on the future growth of the stock price. This future value as predicted may be substantially different from the actual future value.

### Q. 5:15  How should a corporate compensation philosophy be utilized in plan design?

A company's compensation philosophy should be the basis for the design of any long-term incentive plans. This philosophy should be set forth in a statement that documents the operating and organizational values that impact compensation and need to address issues such as:

- How much compensation should be at risk?
- Should organization levels affect how much compensation is at risk?
- How competitive does the organization want/need to be competitive?

Internal organizational values expressed in such a compensation philosophy statement should be as important as what other companies are doing in determining the appropriate design of a long-term plan. An over-emphasis on competitive practices hinders organizations in developing executive compensation programs that support business objectives.

**Planning Tip:** Your plan will probably include the standard corporate intention to "attract, retain and motivate" executives. However, in a practical sense, this is not an adequate basis for a plan design, nor is it a criterion against which plan design can be measured for effectiveness. In determining your compensation philosophy, you need to be far more specific than this.

### Q. 5:16  What is the primary disadvantage of long-term, objectives-based programs?

Experience shows that many companies are unable to forecast beyond a one-year period, with sufficient accuracy, performance standards for incentive purposes. As market, financial and other conditions change over long-term performance periods, executives may become eligible for "windfall" bonuses or conversely, become ineligible for bonuses through unforeseen changes in the business environment. Only where management has a successful track record of longer term forecasting and operates in a relatively stable environment should targets be established over a longer period.

### Q. 5:17  How do companies typically determine the amount of the long-term incentive payout or grant?

Two basic methods are used to establish the potential payout amount of the long-term plan. These two methods are the income-test approach and the salary-multiple test. The income test is used by many companies. Under the income-test approach, target income levels are established for various positions. Option levels, or grant amounts, are then calculated so that if business performance objectives are achieved, executives will obtain the targeted long-term income levels. The difficulty with this approach is that the volatility of the stock market has made it difficult to predict stock price movements. Even in nonstock-based, long-term incentive plans, it is difficult to predict long-term company performance.

The salary-multiple approach is more frequently used to determine appropriate grant levels. This approach expresses stock option or other awards as a ratio of total current market price at time of grant to the participant's salary and assumes that over a wide range of companies, stock appreciation opportunities are related to the stock price at the date of grant. The drawback of this approach is that knowing that an executive has received stock options whose exercise price is 75 percent of his or her base salary does not provide information on the real value of the grant.

In some cases, companies choose not to utilize these methods and make individual decisions for each executive. In the absence of a predetermined formula, these individual decisions are based typically on previous grant amounts and how well the company is currently performing. However, because of the long-term nature of these programs, it has always been difficult to determine whether at any specific time a given capital accumulation program is competitive. Therefore, most companies focus their plan design more internally and determine capital accumulation amounts using the standard methods.

It is generally accepted that a CEO of a publicly-traded company should own stock equal to 10 to 20 times his or her cash compensation. It is generally accepted that with such an ownership position, a corresponding change in the executive's net worth of 100 to 200 percent will result when there is a change in the value of the employer's stock equal to plus or minus 10 percent, which is the level of risk that focuses the executive's actions on managing the business from the perspective of a long-term shareholder.

### Q. 5:18   What is a stock option?

A stock option is the right to buy a share of stock at a predetermined price during a predetermined time period.

### Q. 5:19   What are the different types of stock options?

The two primary categories of stock options are "statutory" options, also known as incentive stock options (ISOs) and "nonstatutory" options, which include all other types of options. These categories are essentially creatures of the Code, which prescribes different tax treatment for the types. Statutory options are governed by Code Sections 421 and 422 while nonstatutory are governed by Code Section 83.

### Q. 5:20   What is the typical exercise period for a stock option?

The typical maximum exercise period for stock options is ten years. Incentive stock options (ISOs) by law are required to have a ten-year exercise period and while there is no requirement that other options contain the same limits, most nonstatutory plans have the ten-year provision.

There are several good reasons for not adhering to the ten-year limit. One reason is that the longer the option's term, the greater the benefit to the executive holding the option because the executive will have greater flexibility in determining when to exercise the stock option for tax and financial planning purposes as well as for market timing. Furthermore, some companies have elected to extend the typical ten-year exercise period, and provide "evergreen" option terms that do not expire until after the executive's retirement. Such an approach provides flexibility to the executive in determining when to exercise the stock option for tax and financial planning purposes as well as for market timing. For example, this type of option incentive would expire on the later of (a) three years after retirement or (b) ten years after grant.

Note, however, that a common oversight which has now been corrected in many plans, but still exists in some, is to have options expire immediately upon retirement, death, or some other event. This does not recognize that many retiring executives (and their estates) need time to make the necessary tax and financial planning arrangements that follow from retirement or death. Nor does such a provision recognize that the market price for the company stock could be artificially depressed at that particular time. As a result many option plans have now been amended to provide for a three or even five-year period after retirement, death or disability during which the option may be exercised.

**Planning Tip:** An option plan should only be amended as to future grants of options, as any changes to the terms of an outstanding option will be considered as a new grant of an option for purposes of the Section 16 rule.

### Q. 5:21   What is the rationale behind using stock-based plans?

As a long-term incentive, the economic benefit to an executive of a stock-based plan can be duplicated through the use of a cash-based plan. However, it is much cheaper for the employer-company to use stock in compensating its executives than it is to pay them the cash value of that stock. Specifically, it is far cheaper for a company to give an executive a share of stock than it is to pay him or her the value of the same share five years later in cash. This is true for two reasons. The first is because shares of stock are "free" to a company while cash is not (ignoring, for purposes of this example, the dilutive impact of the issuance of shares). The second is because if the company has achieved its goals, the stock should be worth far more over time. Also gains that are generated by nonqualified stock option and restricted stock option plans above the fair market value at the date of grant do not produce a charge to earnings but can provide a company with a deduction.

In addition, publicly-traded corporations like to use stock-based plans because this enables them to plan a large block of stock in "friendly" hands, which makes takeover attempts more difficult. Privately-held corporations can also benefit from using stock-based plans as a way of gradually transferring ownership or voting control.

### Q. 5:22   Under what conditions are stock options effective?

For a stock-option plan to be effective, the company's stock must be consistently appreciating, or have sufficient fluctuation that the grant price becomes less than the market price during the period in which the option is exercisable. Option plans in companies that have slow or negligible stock appreciation tend not to provide any motivation to executives.

### Q. 5:23  Where are stock options ineffective?

Stock options in mature companies with poor stock price growth potential are neither an effective retention nor motivational tool. Stock options in highly cyclical industries are not necessarily an effective motivational tool because much of the gain in the price of stock is due to circumstances beyond the executive's control, although they may be an effective retention factor during the growth portion of the cycle if most of the benefits are tied to continued employment. In addition, if executives do not have sufficient cash resources to hold the purchased stock, the traditional objective of tying executives to shareholder interests is not achieved.

### Q. 5:24  How do companies determine how many shares to reserve for stock option plans?

There is no formula that is consistently used in this process although practice has shown that three factors affect the number or shares reserved for long-term plans. These factors are:

1.  Industry;
2.  Size of the company's capitalization; and
3.  The company's state in its life cycle.

In general, companies reserve between 5 percent and 10 percent of their outstanding stock for stock option plans although higher capitalized companies tend to reserve fewer shares than normal. High-risk companies like those that result from leveraged buyouts and start-up companies usually allocate higher percentages to their stock option plans, possibly to make it more palatable for executives to tolerate (and/or reward for) the risk involved in those situations.

### Q. 5:25  What is an omnibus plan?

An omnibus plan is a long-term stock based incentive plan design that normally encompasses almost every conceivable form of capital accumulation plan. The rationale for such a broad-based plan is the avoidance of having to go back to shareholders to get approval for a new capital accumulation plan. These plans generally authorize the issuance of a total number of shares to be used from any or all or a combination of stock plans.

For example, an omnibus plan could provide for grants of non-qualified stock options, restricted stock grants, performance units, discounted stock and SARs. After the plan is approved by the shareholders, the company's compensation committee can use any of the vehicles to reward executives. Before each grant cycle issues such as stock price movement, both current and anticipated, would be reviewed to determine which vehicles were the most feasible. Frequently, executives at different levels in the organization would receive different forms of the long-term incentive.

One concern about omnibus plans is that they are too general and may not provide sufficient information to shareholders who must approve them.

### Q. 5:26  What are some of the tax concepts involved in a long-term incentive plan?

How benefits under a long-term incentive plan are taxed will depend on the application of the various Code rules governing the transfer of property to an employee as compensation for services, which are based in part on the doctrine of constructive receipt and the related economic benefit theory.

### Q. 5:27  What is the general tax impact of a long-term incentive plan?

Compensation payments constitute income to the executive and a deduction to the company in the year in which they are actually or constructively made. With cash-based plans, the timing is relatively clear. On the other hand, with stock-based plans the timing will depend largely on the terms attached to the stock or options. Code Section 83 provides that property transferred to an employee as compensation ("compensatory property"), is not includible in that employee's income until such time as the employee's rights to the property are substantially vested. Property is substantially vested when it is either transferable or not subject to a substantial risk of forfeiture. Upon vesting, the executive must report ordinary income that is equal to the difference between the fair market value of the stock and the amount, if any, paid for it. At this time the company is entitled to a corresponding compensation deduction. For example, Executive A receives shares of restricted stock, which may not be transferred and which will be forfeited upon the occurrence of any number of events, many of which are beyond Executive A's control. The Code recognizes that Executive A has not actually received property and, as a result, does not deem that he has received the property (which would subject him to tax) until his rights to the property are more clearly established. Specifically, when the restrictions that create a substantial risk of forfeiture have lapsed.

### Q. 5:28 What are some of the conditions that create a "substantial risk of forfeiture?"

The most important condition that creates a substantial risk of forfeiture is the conditioning of an executive's right to full enjoyment of the stock or other property, whether directly or indirectly, upon his or her future performance of substantial services to the company. [IRC § 83(c)(1); Treas Reg § 1.83-3(c)(1)] Similarly, conditioning the right to the stock on the company's future performance, for example, an increase in total earnings, will result in the finding that a substantial risk of forfeiture exists.

### Q. 5:29 What are some of the conditions that do not create a "substantial risk of forfeiture?"

For purposes of determining whether stock has substantially vested, a substantial risk of forfeiture will not be found to exist merely because the executive must forfeit shares of the stock or options if convicted of a crime or terminated for-cause, or because the executive accepts a job with a competing firm. Note, however, that the facts in an individual case may show that these restrictions were so strong that they did, in fact, constitute a substantial risk of forfeiture.

### Q. 5:30 What is the general tax effect of a stock option?

There are three different times in the "life" of any stock option at which it may be taxable to the employee. They are (1) at the time it is granted, (2) at the time it is exercised, and (3) on the ultimate disposition of the stock acquired upon its exercise.

*Statutory Options:* For a statutory option, as long as the employee complies with the required holding periods, he or she will incur no tax consequences upon the grant or exercise of the option under Code Section 421 and 422 and the executive will be taxed only when the stock is sold. However, if the fair market value of the underlying stock at the time of the exercise is greater than the option exercise price, the amount of the excess may be a tax preference in calculating the alternative minimum tax.

The tax to the executive at the time of sale is a long-term capital gains tax measured on the difference between the price at which the stock was sold and the exercise price of the stock option. The corporation that granted the option is not entitled to any compensation deduction with respect to the option at any of the three above referenced points because the employee never received compensation income from the option.

*Nonstatutory Options:* For a nonstatutory option, the employee is taxed either at the time of the grant or at the time of exercise and then again when the underlying shares are sold. Generally, at the time of grant the options will be subject to a substantial risk of forfeiture and not currently taxable unless the executive makes an election under Code Section 83 to be taxed immediately. In either case the executive will be deemed to recognize compensation income and the corporation will be entitled to a compensation deduction equal to the amount of income that has accrued to the employee. When the employee sells the underlying shares the gain recognized will be taxed as long-term capital gain.

Furthermore, an executive exercising an option must satisfy federal and state withholding requirements. He or she may do this by paying additional cash to satisfy these requirements, by having the company withhold the required amount from the shares issued upon exercise of the option, or by delivering additional already-owned shares. If shares are used to pay the tax withholding, special Section 16 rules apply in order for the surrender not to be deemed a sale.

### Q. 5:31    What is the doctrine of constructive receipt of income?

As set forth in Q. 5:27, income is to be included in an executive's gross income for the taxable year in which it is actually *or constructively* received. The intent of this concept is to prevent an executive from not accepting earned income solely to avoid current taxation.

Under the theory of constructive receipt, an executive will be subject to tax if he or she has unrestricted control in determining when such income should be received. For example, an executive may be deemed to have constructively received an incentive payment if he/she has an election to receive it currently or defer the payment until a future date.

### Q. 5:32   How does the constructive receipt doctrine impact deferred compensation?

In developing deferred compensation plans, it is crucial that the plan be structured so that the executive cannot be regarded as in constructive receipt of the compensation before the executive actually receives the compensation. *Revenue Ruling 60-31* establishes the primary basis for designing nonqualified deferred compensation plans. This revenue ruling states that amounts paid pursuant to a nonqualified deferred compensation plan will be subject to inclusion in the executive's income only in the taxable years in which the executive receives the payments. In addition, this revenue ruling states that it is not necessary to build in forfeit provisions as long as the plan is entered into before the executive renders his or her services. In designing deferred compensation plans, these safeguards should be included:

- If the decision to defer compensation (rather than receive it currently) is elective on the part of the executive, the executive should make the election prior to the time the services for which the compensation is paid are rendered.

- If the compensation is deferred to some specific or determinable future date, the executive should, as a general rule, not be given a unilateral election to defer it to a still later date once the services have been rendered. For example, if an executive has elected to defer some compensation until age 65, the executive should not have a unilateral second election prior to age 65 to defer its receipt until some later age.

## Q. 5:33   What is the economic benefit theory?

Related to the constructive receipt concept, the "economic bene-fit" doctrine means that when an economic benefit has been granted, and such benefit is equivalent to cash, the executive may be taxed currently. In other words, the executive is taxed when he/she receives something of value which is the equivalent of cash. Normally a mere promise to pay in the future, if it is unfunded and unsecured, is not of sufficient economic benefit to be taxable even if it is nonforfeitable at the time it is made. Whether more than a mere promise is involved in a given situation and if so whether that additional factor creates a taxable economic benefit is an ever present problem raised by the doctrine of economic benefit.

## Q. 5:34   What is a Code Section 83(b) election?

Although the general rule for compensatory property is that rights that are substantially vested are currently taxable while rights that are substantially nonvested are not currently taxable, Code Section 83(b) allows an employee to choose to be taxed immediately on the bargain element received in connection with a substantially nonvested right. This is accomplished by having the executive file an election with IRS that states he or she will pay ordinary income on the bargain element as measured at the time of receipt. Of course, any future appreciation in the property will be treated as a capital gain when sold. This election must be made within 30 days of receiving the stock.

The most significant drawback of the Code Section 83(b) election is that the executive does not receive a tax deduction (or tax loss) if the property is ultimately forfeited. Balancing this against the fact that the difference between ordinary income and capital gains tax rate is presently minimal, an important historical motivation for a Code Section 83(b) election—to obtain capital gains treatment for all the value of the property's appreciation rather than just the appreciation that occurs after the lapse of the restrictions—is not as compelling as it once was.

### Q. 5:35  With the elimination of capital gains, is a Code Section 83(b) election meaningless?

No, even though a primary historical attraction of the 83(b) election was to have stock appreciation taxed as capital gain rather than ordinary income. (With only a slight difference between capital gains rates and ordinary income rates, this distinction is now meaningless because under current tax rules an executive would not file a Code Section 83(b) election because it would subject that executive to immediate tax liability with a potential nondeductible loss if the property was ultimately forfeited.)

Yet, the Code Section 83(b) election retains some value. First, there is the continuing discussion in Congress about reinstating the capital gains rate. If this were to occur, the Code Section 83(b) election would properly position an executive for eventual preferential tax rate treatment. More importantly, the Code Section 83(b) election gives the executive control over the timing of the eventual tax event and where the initial bargain element is small, such as with start-up or high technology companies, no future tax will be due until the stock is actually sold.

### Q. 5:36  What are the different ways an employee can pay the exercise price of a stock option?

There are three primary ways for an employee to pay the exercise price of an option. The three ways are (1) by using cash, (2) by delivering already-owned stock, and (3) by a "cashless exercise." Where an executive delivers shares of already-owned stock, the market value of the stock is applied towards the exercise price. As an example, Executive C has an option to purchase 1,000 shares of Company D stock at an exercise price of $10 per share. If the then-current market price is $25 per share, Executive A can pay the exercise price by delivering 400 shares of stock he already owns.

Until the recent revisions to the Section 16 rules, insiders were limited to the use of cash in order to exercise their options. Now, however, these techniques are available to all employees.

## Q. 5:37   How do the Section 16 rules affect stock plans and the way employees can pay for stock?

Under Section 16 an insider is not allowed to purchase and sell securities within a six-month period. Under prior rules the exercise of an option was considered a purchase of the underlying shares and "matchable" with any other sale by the executive during the six months before or after the date of exercise. As a result, an insider could not pay the option exercise price by tendering already-owned shares because that tender would constitute a sale that would be matched against the purchase that existed by virtue of the exercise of the option.

The recently amended Section 16 rules provide that the exercise of an option is not considered a purchase for purposes of Section 16. Instead, only the acquisition of the option and the disposition of the underlying shares will be events that will be subject to possible Section 16(b) sanctions. Furthermore, the acquisition of the option will be exempt from Section 16(b) if the grant is made pursuant to a plan that fulfills the requirements of Rule 16b-3, the most important of which are that the plan be approved by the company's shareholders and that grants under the plan be administered by disinterested directors. These new rules have significantly liberalized the use of options by insiders by extending them the possibility of paying for their stock through the stock swap, cashless exercises and pyramiding methods. The new rules have also lessened the need for stock appreciation rights (SARs) and other techniques designed to provide insiders with the cash required to exercise their stock options. (Certain new rules deal specifically with SARs and are discussed at Chapter 7.)

However, there are two important exceptions to this liberalization. One involves options that have exercise prices that are not definitely set but, instead, are expressed as percentages of the market price of the stock on the date of exercise. For these types of options the securities will not be deemed to have been acquired for purposes of Section 16 reporting or liability until the exercise or conversion price becomes fixed. The exercise or conversion price usually becomes fixed on the date of exercise. A second exception involves the exercise of out-of-money stock options, which is not an exempt transaction for Section 16(b) purposes because "there generally is no rational economic reason for such exercises." [Exchange Act Rel No 43-28869]

These exceptions are best understood within the underlying rationale for the Section 16 rules, which rests on the belief that an insider should not be able to profit from nonpublic information about his company.

**Example:** Executive E is granted an option to purchase 1,000 shares of Company F stock at $7, and Executive F is granted an option to purchase 1,000 shares at 70% of their fair market value on the date of exercise. Even if E learns of material nonpublic information that could be expected to cause the stock to increase, he has no opportunity to use it (in the context of his option) because his profit has been set. Executive F would be able to share in the stock's increase only if he exercised the option immediately, because his exercise price increases with the market value if he waits. This is precisely the situation that the Section 16 rules seek to prevent.

### Q. 5:38  What is a cashless option exercise?

Federal Reserve Board, Regulation T, of the NASD Rules permits broker-dealers to treat an option exercise notice as if it were stock, and, as a result, to advance funds to the executive in order to pay for the exercise of the option. This is called the "cashless exercise" of stock options. It is called "cashless" because the executive can pay the exercise price for the stock with the proceeds of the sale of the underlying shares. The process involves delivering an irrevocable exercise notice to the executive's broker that instructs the company to deliver the stock that is subject to the option to the broker. Note that traditional margin requirements are applicable to the cashless option exercise unless the stock is immediately sold.

### Q. 5:39  What is Regulation T and how does it impact executive compensation?

Regulation T impacts executive compensation because it affects how an executive can finance the exercise of options or sale of stock through a brokerage account. Specifically, the amount a customer must deposit in a margin account and conversely the amount the broker may lend is prescribed by the Board of Governors at the

Federal Reserve Board by authority of the Securities Exchange Act of 1934 under Regulation T.

### Q. 5:40   What is a stock swap?

A stock swap is another name for the method of delivering already-owned stock to exercise a stock option. Instead of the executive paying cash to exercise a stock option, a stock swap involves exchanging already-owned stock to pay for the stock option which the executive exercises.

### Q. 5:41   What is a pyramiding exercise?

Pyramiding is an extension of a stock swap that involves a series of stock swaps enabling the executive to keep exchanging stock in and for ever increasing amounts.

**Example:** Executive A owns one share of stock with a market value of $50. The executive also has an option to buy 200 shares at an option price of $10 per share. The executive could turn in the one share worth $50 in order to exercise a portion of his option, as to five shares at $10 per share. He would then surrender those five shares, valued at $250, to exercise his option as to 25 shares, which have a market value of $1,250 (25 shares at $50), and then surrender those 25 shares to exercise his option as to 125 shares, and then surrender 9 shares to exercise his option as to the remaining 45 shares. At the end of the process, he would have 161 shares worth $8,050. (This example ignores for illustrative purposes the tax withholding requirement.)

### Q. 5:42   What is the tax treatment for a stock swap or pyramiding?

The impact of a stock swap or pyramiding exercise depends on whether the stock option is a statutory or a nonstatutory option.

*Nonstatutory Options:* With a nonstatutory option the exchange of already-owned shares for the same number of shares is a tax-free exchange. The fair market value of any additional shares received is taxable income to the executive and the company does not recognize any gain or loss on the exchange.

*Statutory Options:* With a statutory stock option (incentive stock option), the exchange is tax free if the shares the executive owns have been held for the required holding period. If the holding period has not been met, the executive will be taxed on the bargain element of the already owned shares as well as any post-exercise appreciation. Regardless of whether the holding period has been met the executive will not be taxed at the time of exercise on the amount by which the value of the newly-acquired shares exceeds the value of the already-owned shares and the company will not recognize a gain or loss on the transaction.

### Q. 5:43   Are there drawbacks to a pyramiding exercise or stock swap?

Yes. Remember that any shares surrendered by an insider to the company to satisfy the exercise price are deemed to have been sold for purposes of Section 16, and are therefore matchable against any other purchases by that insider during the preceding and succeeding six months. Furthermore, if the plan is already in place and does not permit payment by stock, then the plan would have to be amended and certain formalities would have to be followed. (See Questions 5:44 and 5:45.)

The other major drawback of pyramiding is the requirement that companies take an accounting charge when options are exercised with shares that are not mature.

### Q. 5:44   What is needed to institute a long-term incentive plan?

Except where a statutory or incentive stock option plan is involved, as long as a corporation has enough authorized but unissued shares to implement a long-term plan and the Board of Directors has been given the right to authorize the issuance of any authorized but unissued shares, the board may either make grants of stock or adopt a formal stock plan and grant shares or options up to the number of authorized but unissued shares or adopt a stock-based plan such as a SAR or phantom stock plan and grant rights thereunder, all without shareholder approval. As a practical matter however, a publicly-traded company will want to obtain shareholder approval for a plan, including a SAR or phantom stock plan, so that grants under that plan will not be matchable transactions for purposes of the Section 16 rules. Furthermore, a privately-held company will want to obtain shareholder approval as a courtesy to the owner-managers.

Special rules apply to statutory, or incentive, stock option plans because they must meet certain conditions in order for the executive to receive preferred tax treatment. Among these conditions is the requirement that the plan be approved by a company's shareholders. However, note that one single plan, often called an "omnibus plan," may be adopted to provide for the grant of more than one form of long-term incentive, including incentive stock options. Additionally, the approval of the shareholders at the time of adoption of the omnibus plan is adequate for the incentive stock option (ISO) rules (assuming that the omnibus plan contemplates the granting of ISOs).

Once a plan has been adopted and approved, the board (or a disinterested committee of the board in the case of public companies wishing to qualify for the Rule 16b-3 exception to the Section 16 rules) makes grants under the plan periodically or as desired in order to compensate its employees. (The use of a disinterested committee of the board to perform this administrative function is discussed in detail in Chapter 11.)

### Q. 5:45    What is needed to amend a long-term incentive plan?

In general, any requirement necessary to adopt a plan is necessary to materially amend it. The Section 16 rules specifically provide that if the amendment is one which would "(A) materially increase the benefits accruing to participants in the plan; (B) materially increase the number of securities which may be issued under the plan; or (C) materially modify the requirements as to eligibility for participation in the plan" then shareholder approval would be required or the Rule 16b-3 exemption would be lost.

### Q. 5:46    What information about a long-term incentive plan must be disclosed in a company's proxy statement?

Any capital accumulation plan utilizing stock must comply with certain proxy disclosure rules both when the plan or any amendment to the plan is submitted to the shareholders for their approval as well as on an ongoing basis.

If shareholders are being requested to adopt or amend any plan pursuant to which cash or noncash compensation may be paid, the details of the plan or the amendment must be set forth in detail together with an explanation of the effects of the various provisions of the proposal. Furthermore, Schedule 14A requires additional disclosures as to all plans. Specifically, the company must disclose information concerning the amounts paid or set aside during the last three years for executive officers and directors under all existing plans. In addition, the company must also disclose the amounts that would have been paid or set aside during the last prior fiscal year if the amendments or plan on which the shareholders are being requested to act had been in effect.

On an ongoing basis, information on the number of options granted and exercised or restricted stock grants paid, distributed or accrued during the most recent fiscal year must be disclosed in each proxy statement as well as the net value of stock received as a result of the exercised stock options.

The specific items of compensation that must be disclosed and the form that the disclosure must take are set forth in Regulation S-K. In general, the proxy materials must also include a brief description of all plans from which payments were made or proposed to be made to the executive officers in the last fiscal year. A summary of how the plan operates must also be provided and should include who is eligible to participate in the plan, payment schedules, recent material plan amendments, and the criteria for determining amounts to be paid, including any performance formula or measure. Information need not be provided for plans such as discriminatory group life, health or relocation plans that are provided to all salaried employees. In short, the proxy statement must include all information that would enable a shareholder to make a determination as to whether the compensation paid to the company's executives was reasonable in amount.

# Chapter 6

# Purchase Plans

Purchase plans are the most frequently used long-term incentive plan design. Purchase plans come in many forms and this chapter covers (1) incentive stock options (ISOs), (2) nonstatutory stock options, (3) restricted stock purchase plans, (4) book value purchase plans, (5) discounted nonstatutory options, and (6) junior stock plans. As a result, purchase plans, which require the executive to make an actual investment, give the executive the opportunity to purchase stock immediately or grant options to purchase stock at a future date. This chapter examines the tax, legal and financial implications of purchase plans as well as their relative strengths and weaknesses.

### Q. 6:1  What is a purchase plan?

Purchase plans are capital accumulation plans that give the executive the opportunity to purchase stock immediately or grant options to purchase stock at a future date.

### Q. 6:2  What are the different types of Purchase Plans?

The main forms of purchase plans, all of which will be discussed in this chapter, are as follows:

- Statutory (incentive) stock option plans;
- Nonstatutory stock option plans, including discount stock option plans, and premium stock option plans;

- Plans based directly on the acquisition of stock rather than options, including restricted stock purchase plans and book value purchase plans; and
- Convertible plans, such as convertible debenture plans, junior stock plans.

### Q. 6:3   What are the fundamental differences between different types of purchase plans?

Purchase plans are similar in that they provide a way for a company to compensate employees with stock. Purchase plans differ primarily in how they accomplish that goal of compensating employees with stock, the tax treatment of the specific transaction, and the amount of investment required of the employee.

### Q. 6:4   How are option exercise prices set?

The most common approach to setting an option exercise price is to set that price at the market value of the stock at the time of grant. Discounted stock options are stock options with exercise prices that are below the market value of the stock at the time of grant, which gives the executive more upside appreciation potential. Conversely, premium stock options establish the option exercise price at a value that is above the current market value of the stock at the time of grant.

### Q. 6:5   How long is the typical options exercise period?

The typical maximum exercise period is ten years.

### Q. 6:6   What is an incentive stock option (ISO)?

ISOs were created by the Economic Recovery Act of 1981 (ERTA) and the requirements that apply to them were modified by the Tax Reform Act of 1986. As a result, ISOs are required to meet the statutory requirements of Code Section 422, which provides that:

1. The ISO may be granted only to an employee of the issuing company, its parent, or a subsidiary of the issuing parent;
2. The ISO must be granted pursuant to a plan that specifies the total number of shares that may be issued under options and the employees (or class of employees) that are eligible to receive options and this plan must be approved by the com-

pany's stockholders within 12 months before or after the date
that the plan is adopted;

3. The ISO, by its terms and at the time it is granted, cannot
   provide that it will not be treated as an ISO;

4. The ISO, by its terms, cannot be exercisable after the expiration
   of ten years from the date that the option is granted and the
   ISO may not be exercisable after the expiration of five years
   from the date the option is granted, if the optionee owns stock
   comprising more than ten percent of the total combined voting
   power of all classes of stock of the company (or parent or
   subsidiary thereof);

5. The ISO, by its terms, cannot be transferable by the optionee
   other than by will or the laws of descent and distribution and
   during the optionee's lifetime, the option may only be exercised by the optionee;

6. The ISO exercise price must not be less that the "fair market
   value" of the stock on the date of the grant, which must be
   determined without regard to any restriction other than a
   restriction that, by its terms, will never lapse, and the ISO
   exercise price must not be less than 10 percent more than the
   fair market value if the optionee owns stock comprising more
   than 10 percent of the total combined voting power of all classes
   of stock of the company (or parent or subsidiary);

7. The option will not be treated as an ISO to the extent that the
   total fair market value (determined at the time of the grant) of
   the stock with respect to which the ISOs are exercisable for the
   first time by any individual during any calendar year exceeds
   $100,000. The determinations are made with regard to all plans
   of the corporation, its parent and subsidiary corporations;

8. The optionee cannot transfer shares acquired upon the exercise of an ISO within two years from the date the option is
   granted or one year from the date the option is exercised and
   the optionee must exercise the option within three months of
   termination of employment, except in cases of death or disability.

Lastly, an ISO may be disqualified as an ISO if care is not taken in
forming the plan. An ISO cannot be paired with an SAR unless the
SAR meets certain requirements (see Q. 7:4), and no change may be
made in the benefit provided by the ISO, so that, for example, an ISO

cannot be amended to add a reload feature, change the payment terms, or extend the exercise period.

## Q. 6:7    What is the tax treatment for an ISO?

The company is allowed no deduction for either the grant of an ISO, the exercise of an ISO, or the sale of the underlying shares.

The executive does not recognize income upon the grant of an ISO, nor from its exercise and the executive has a taxable event only when the underlying shares are sold.

If an executive transfers shares acquired on the exercise of an ISO within two years after the date of grant of the ISO or within one year after receiving those shares (either of which is often referred to as a "disqualifying distribution", he or she disqualifies the option as an ISO and therefore loses the favorable tax treatment. In that event, the executive will realize ordinary income in the year of the disqualification in an amount equal to the difference between the option price and the fair market value of the stock on the date of exercise. The balance of the gain on that disposition remains capital gain and the corporation, of course, would be entitled to deduct the amount of income taxed to the employee in the year in which the employee realizes the income, although it is difficult in practice for a company to keep track of disqualifying dispositions.

**Example:** On July 1, 1989, Kristina was granted an ISO for 1,000 shares of Gable company stock. The exercise price is $20, which was the current value of the stock on the date of grant. On November 1, 1990, Kristina exercised her option to purchase the 1,000 shares when the current fair market value was $24 by paying $20,000 ($20 × 1,000 shares). In December, 1991, Kristina sells her 1,000 shares for the current market value of $28,000. Because Kristina has satisfied the two holding period requirements by not selling the stock within two years of the grant (July 1, 1989) or within one year of the exercise (November 1, 1990), she is entitled to capital gain treatment on the $800 spread between the grant price and the sales price.

Gable corporation does not receive a tax deduction when the option is granted in 1989 nor when it is exercised in 1990 nor when sold in 1991.

### Q. 6:8   How does the alternative minimum tax impact the tax treatment of an ISO?

The optionee may be subject to the alternative minimum tax ("AMT") in the year he exercises an ISO because the exercise of an ISO gives rise to an adjustment of AMT income equal to the difference between the fair market value of the stock at the exercise date and the exercise price of the option for purposes of applying the Code Section 83 rules. Similarly, any gain on the stock after exercise of the option will be calculated for AMT purposes. This gain will be measured by determining the difference between the sale price and the exercise price as adjusted by the amount of the AMT income adjustment at the time of exercise.

### Q. 6:9   What is the accounting impact of an ISO?

The company does not recognize any expense in connection with the grant of an ISO, either at the time of grant or upon the exercise of the ISO. However, outstanding ISOs are considered to be common stock equivalents, so that the number of shares subject to the option are factored into a determination of per share earnings.

### Q. 6:10   What approach is used in calculating the fully diluted earnings per share for an ISO?

The ISO effect on fully diluted earnings per share is computed in the same manner as for the primary earnings per share except that if the common stock price is higher than the average market price during the period, the higher price is used in the computation.

### Q. 6:11   How prevalent are ISOs?

While incentive stock options exist in the majority of publicly-traded companies, few companies are currently installing ISOs. Over time, ISOs will disappear as a capital accumulation method in all but a few circumstances because the favorable individual tax advantages associated with ISOs were eliminated by TRA '86. Prior to 1986, incentive stock options provided favorable tax treatment to executives in two ways. First, the gains were not taxable at exercise and second, the gains were taxable at capital gains rates.

## Q. 6:12   Under what circumstances does an ISO still make sense?

The ISO continues to make sense to the executive because of its financial planning feature, in that the ISO permits the executive to choose when the taxable event will occur because the ISO generates taxable income only when it is sold. ISOs can make sense from the company's perspective when the company is at a low or zero effective tax bracket and does not need a tax deduction. Where this is the case, the ISOs lack of deductibility, the primary disadvantage of ISOs, is negated.

## Q. 6:13   What are the advantages of an ISO?

The primary advantage of an ISO is that the executive does not recognize income on either the grant or the exercise of the ISO. Therefore, the executive controls the taxable event. In other words, the executive can determine when he or she will generate the tax liability because the executive determines when the acquired stock will actually be sold.

Income received from the sale of ISO stock is still taxed to the executive as capital gains although the tax rate is virtually the same as ordinary income rates. The advantage of this characterization is that the gain realized may be offset by any capital losses and the possibility that a lower capital gains rate may be reintroduced remains.

**Planning Tip:** Companies with ISOs may want to encourage executives to make "disqualifying dispositions" of the stock so that the company can receive a tax deduction in the amount of the gain attributed to the executive. A company can encourage this by offering executives who dispose of their stock and incur a tax liability a bonus or a tax-offset bonus.

## Q. 6:14   What are the primary disadvantages of an ISO?

From a company perspective, the primary disadvantage of an ISO is the lack of a company tax deduction when the executive exercises the option, which causes the grant of an ISO to be a relatively expensive compensation vehicle to the company.

## Q. 6:15  What is a nonstatutory stock option?

A nonstatutory option is any option that does not meet the requirements of an ISO. Nonstatutory stock options are sometimes referred
to as "nonqualified" options or "NQSOs" because the tax-preferred
predecessor to the statutory/incentive stock option was the
"qualified" stock option. There are two basic types of nonstatutory
options, (1) options that have a readily ascertainable value when
granted, and (2) options that do not. In order for an option to have
a readily ascertainable market value, it must either itself be tradable
on a securities exchange or must be immediately exercisable and
subject to no further restrictions; in that event, the value of the option
is compensation to the executive at the time received. This is a
compensation device that is almost never used by a corporation in a
long-term plan, as it does not tie the executive's long-term reward to
his future service to the company. (Note that the devices relating to
stock options discussed throughout this book concentrate on nonstatutory options that do not have a readily ascertainable market
value.)

## Q. 6:16  How prevalent are nonstatutory stock options?

Nonstatutory stock option plans are the most common form of
capital accumulation programs and between 50 percent and 60 percent of publicly-traded companies offer nonstatutory stock options
(NQSOs) to their executives. Prior to TRA '86, NQSOs tended to be
less prevalent because tax-favored options such as ISOs were available.
Since the elimination of the favorable aspects of ISOs, nonstatutory
stock options have grown considerably in usage and should continue
to grow in the future because even if the tax-favored options should
rebound as the result of a lowered capital gains rate, companies will
still use NQSOs to overcome the various limitations that are placed
on tax-favored options.

## Q. 6:17  What is the accounting impact of a nonstatutory stock option?

Where a nonstatutory option is granted at the market price, the
company has no accounting compensation charge at the time of
grant, at the exercise of the option, or at the sale of the underlying

shares. However, in the case of an option granted below the market, such as a discount stock option, the company must recognize compensation expense upon the exercise of the option in the amount of the spread.

The company's earnings per share are diluted because stock options are common stock equivalents, and thus the EPS calculation assumes that all outstanding stock options were exercised. The EPS calculation also assumes that the monies received by the company upon the exercise of the options would be used to repurchase shares in the open market. Each year until the options are either exercised or expire, the impact on earnings per share will be lessened when market values are approximately the same as the exercise price.

**Example:** Company G has granted options to its executives to purchase an aggregate of 10,000 shares of stock at $10; the market value of the shares is 25. The net dilutive effect is 6,000 shares, since the Company could purchase 4,000 shares on the open market if all the options were exercised. If the market value of Company G's stock were $11, the dilutive effect would be only 909 shares since the company could purchase 9,090 shares of stock.

### Q. 6:18   What is the tax treatment of a nonstatutory stock option?

For a nonstatutory option, the employee is taxed either at the time of grant or the time of exercise, and then again when he sells the underlying shares. Generally, at the time of grant the options will be subject to a substantial risk of forfeiture, and thus not currently taxable, unless the executive makes an election under Code Section 83(b) to be taxed immediately. In either case he will be deemed to recognize compensation income in the amount of the spread, and the corporation will be entitled to a compensation deduction in the amount of income that accrued to the employee. When the employee sells the underlying shares, the gain recognized will be taxed as a capital gain.

### Q. 6:19   What are the advantages of nonstatutory options?

Most companies find nonstatutory options appealing as a result of the greater flexibility afforded them in designing a long-term incentive plan. Unlike statutory options, nonstatutory stock options can be granted in any (read greater) amount, and can have exercise prices lower than the fair market value of the stock on the date of the option grant

### Q. 6:20  What are the disadvantages of nonstatutory stock options?

With nonstatutory stock options, the optionee is taxed at the time the option is exercised (or upon the grant of the option if the optionee has so elected), so there is no deferral of recognition as there is with an ISO. Similarly, the corporation is required to withhold with respect to the income recognized by the optionee. This can result in a real burden to the employee who does not intend to immediately dispose of the stock acquired upon exercise of the option.

This problem used to be even worse for insiders, who, because of potential Section 16 liability, could not immediately sell stock to pay for the exercise of their options. To ease this added burden, Code Section 83 contains a provision permitting an insider to defer taxation for as long as six months if the sale of the stock acquired upon exercise of the option would subject the holder to Section 16 liability. However, the adoption of the new Section 16 rules, permitting an insider to exercise an option and sell shares immediately, has made this accommodating provision unnecessary.

### Q. 6:21  Can features be added to nonstatutory stock options to offset the withholding burden?

Yes. The two methods most often used in dealing with the withholding and payment burdens are the following:

1. The corporation can provide a cash bonus on exercise. (A variation on this method involves the use of a tandem stock option/stock appreciation right, discussed in Chapter 9.)

2. The corporation can withhold from the number of shares issuable upon exercise of the option that number of shares necessary to satisfy the withholding requirement, or can accept from the employee a larger number of shares of stock in a stock-for-stock exercise.

Where an insider is involved, Section 16 has an impact if one of these methods is chosen. A cash bonus payable upon the exercise of an option, even if not a formal tandem stock option/SAR, and the decision to have issuable shares withheld, are each deemed to be SARs and subject to special rules: the exercise must be made during the "window period" or the withheld shares will be deemed to have been sold for purposes of Section 16 liability (see Q. 7:4).

### Q. 6:22  How do ISOs compare with nonstatutory stock options?

The principal benefit of the ISO accrues to the executive who is entitled to capital gains treatment of the full value of the grant. This benefit was eliminated, however, with the elimination of truly favorable capital gains tax rates. The only remaining advantage to using ISOs is again from the employee's perspective, that is, the opportunity for the executive to defer the taxable event until the sale of the underlying shares. In most cases, this will not outweigh the significant cost to the company of losing a deduction for compensation expense.

### Q. 6:23  What is a discounted stock option (DSO)?

Although a discounted stock option is technically any nonstatutory option with an exercise price that is lower than the fair market value of the stock at the time of grant, the term usually refers to an option with an exercise price that is fixed at a substantial discount from the fair market value on the date of grant. Frequently, these plans are utilized for compensating outside members of the Board of Directors (see Chapter 11). Traditionally, a DSO has been used to encourage immediate ownership and to protect against drops in the market price. To reinforce the ownership element, the purchased stock is sometimes subject to some holding period and/or tenure restrictions. For example, the shares acquired under such a plan may not be sold for a certain period after the purchase or must be resold to the company at the discounted price if the executive terminates employment prior to a specified date.

**Example:** Anne is an executive of Gable corporation, which grants her an option for 1,000 shares of its stock on August 18, 1988. The exercise price of the option is $5, which is one-half the market value of $10. On September 1, 1989, the current value of the stock is $14 and Anne decides to exercise her option and purchase 1,000 shares for $5,000. For 1989, Anne has $9,000 of reportable income, which is computed as follows:

| | |
|---|---|
| Value of the stock | $14,000 ($14 × 1,000) |
| Purchase price | (5,000) |
| Reportable Income | $ 9,000 |

Gable corporation receives a corresponding $9,000 tax deduction. In October, 1991, Anne sells the 1,000 shares at $20 per share and reports a $6,000 taxable capital gain; Gable is not entitled to a deduction for that gain.

The exercise price for discounted stock options is generally expressed as a fixed price, although it is more rarely expressed as a percentage of market value at the time of exercise. If the exercise price is allowed to vary with the market price, the executive is at a real disadvantage for purposes of the Section 16 rules as he or she will not be deemed to have acquired the shares until the option is actually exercised. (See Q. 5:37.)

### Q. 6:24 How prevalent are discount stock option plans?

DSOs are becoming prevalent as a mechanism for deferral of income for directors (see Chapter 11). These are used infrequently as a compensation mechanism for executives.

### Q. 6:25 What is the tax treatment for a discount stock option?

The tax consequences resulting from the grant and exercise of a discount stock option are the same as those applicable to nonstatutory options in general. Absent a Section 83(b) election, the discounted option is not compensation to the executive when granted, but becomes income upon its exercise recognizable by the employee and deductible by the corporation.

### Q. 6:26 What is the accounting impact of a discount stock option?

Unlike the normal treatment for nonstatutory options granted at market prices, the company must take a charge to earnings in the amount of the discount.

## Q. 6:27   What are the advantages of a discount stock option plan?

The primary advantage of a discount stock plan is the "cushion" provided an executive if the stock price falls and the built-in appreciation or gain the executive receives is diminished. A discount stock option is also a way to effectively defer compensation, as no taxable income will be generated to the executive (absent an 83(b) election) until the option is exercised. (See Chapter 11 for the advantages for the director's compensation deferral.)

## Q. 6:28   What are the disadvantages of a discount stock option plan?

The most often voiced criticism of a discount stock plan is that the executive receives a reward even if the stock price does not appreciate or does not depreciate more than the discount.

Under a discount stock option plan, even decreasing stock prices can generate large rewards.

**Example:** Executive B received 10,000 discount stock options as part of the recruitment process. The option price was $34 and the current stock price was $68. Three years later when B exercised the options, the stock price had declined to $52 per share. At that point executive B still received $180,000 ($54 – $34 × 10,000) for "managing" the stock price down by $16 per share.

A second disadvantage is the requirement that the company must reflect the benefit provided to the executive in the discount of the exercise price at the time of grant of the option as compensation expense for accounting purposes even though it is not entitled to the corresponding tax benefit until the option is exercised.

Another potential problem with discount stock options is the depth of the discount, because at some point the grant of a deeply discounted option becomes the transfer of the underlying shares. However, instead of granting an executive an option to purchase a small number of shares at a deeply discounted price, a company can give the same initial benefit to an executive by granting him an option to purchase a larger number of shares at a price that is not so deeply discounted.

**Example:** In the above example, Executive B had received 10,000 discount stock options with an exercise price of $34 versus the $64 market price; the value of the benefit granted to him at that time by the company was $340,000. If Company C had granted him 25,000 options with an exercise price of $50, the immediate spread would have been $350,000. In that case, he would have received only $50,000 upon the sale of the underlying shares after the company's dismal performance during the three years he held them.

### Q. 6:29  How deeply can discounted stock options be discounted?

IRS has avoided issuing regulations on the point at which a deeply discounted option would be considered to be a "sham" option and recharacterized as a transfer of the underlying stock, taxable immediately as income to the recipient. Recently, an executive who received discounted options with an exercise price equal to the par value of the stock, $1, to purchase company shares whose appraised value was $143 per share, was hit with a huge tax liability when IRS determined that the grant was in fact a transfer of the underlying shares.

As a practical matter, discounts of more than 50 percent begin to expose the company and the executive to this kind of recharacterization. A company considering deeply discounted stock would be wise to consider getting a private letter ruling from IRS on the appropriateness of the discount.

### Q. 6:30  What is a premium stock option?

A premium stock option permits an executive to purchase company stock at specified periods (i.e., five or ten years) at a price above the current market price at the time the option is granted. The "premium" attached to the current price of the stock option is typically the normal expected growth in the company's stock price and serves as a threshold level to guarantee that the company perform at a certain level before an executive can benefit.

The exercise price can either be set at the same premium during the entire life of the option, or increase by a specified rate from year to year.

**Example:** Kristina is an executive with Gable corporation and on July 1, 1986 when the market value of the stock was $10 she is granted an option to purchase 1,000 shares of stock at an exercise price that would change from year to year as follows:

| | |
|---|---|
| 1986 | $10.60 |
| 1987 | $11.24 |
| 1988 | $11.91 |
| 1989 | $12.62 |

When the market value of the stock reached $15 on February 1, 1989, Kristina exercised her option and acquired 1,000 shares for $11,910 (1,000 shares × $11.91). For 1989, Kristina recognizes ordinary income, computed as follows:

| | |
|---|---|
| Value of stock | $15,000 |
| Amount paid | (11,910) |
| Amount of ordinary income | 3,190 |

Gable corporation is entitled to a tax deduction for the $3,190 that Kristina recognized as income.

On February 1, 1992, Kristina sells the 1,000 shares at the then current market value of $16 and she recognizes capital gain, computed as follows:

| | |
|---|---|
| Proceeds of sale | $16,000 |
| Basis in stock | (15,000) |
| Amount of capital gain | 1,000 |

Gable corporation is not entitled to a deduction even though Kristina has recognized a taxable gain of $1,000.

## Q. 6:31 How is the premium established?

There are several ways to establish the premium although the most common methods are the Treasury Bill (T-Bill) and the peer-group methods. The T-bill method is intended to reflect the cost of capital so that an executive may, for example, receive an option for 1,000 shares at a $74.75 exercise price when the current market value is $38. Assuming that the T-bill return is seven percent, the $38 stock price would eventually reach the $74.75 exercise price over ten years. The rationale for this approach is that the executive should not profit unless the executive can make the company outperform a low-risk investment such as Treasury bonds.

A second approach, as noted above, is the peer-group approach, which is most appropriate for publicly-traded companies and those companies with easily identifiable competitors because this approach focuses on relative performance against competitor firms. For example, consider an airline company stock that is traded at $80 that wants to establish the price at which an option would be exercisable after five years. It would multiply $80 (the current price) by the industry average stock price appreciation. If the industry average stock growth rate was 10 percent over five years, the exercise price would then be established at $88. The peer-group approach emphasizes that an executive should not be rewarded if his or her company's stock price does not at least out-perform the average rate of performance within its industry peer groups. As a result, in this example, if the company's stock price moved 20 percent upward to $96, which exceeds the predetermined average, the executive would exercise that option at $88 and would profit $8 per option. However, if the company stock price moved only 10 percent (the industry average) the executive could still exercise the option and purchase shares, although he or she would receive no immediate reward or gain.

### Q. 6:32 How prevalent are premium stock options?

Premium stock options are not common among companies although several large companies have implemented these plans in the last year.

### Q. 6:33 What is the accounting impact of a premium stock option?

There is no financial accounting impact for a premium stock option grant.

### Q. 6:34 What is the tax treatment for a premium stock option?

There is no tax effect to the corporation or to the executive at the time a premium stock option is granted. The corporation, however, is entitled to a deduction equal to the amount that is taxable when the executive receives the income that is ordinary income equal to the spread between the option exercise price and the fair market value of the shares. Because the spread is taxable as ordinary income, the company is required to withhold taxes.

### Q. 6:35   For what type of company does a premium stock option make sense?

This type of plan appeals to companies that believe that an executive should only be rewarded if the company stock appreciates more than a certain amount. Furthermore, a premium stock option plan will pay out only if there is an active market for the stock and the stock appreciates.

### Q. 6:36   What is an option reload plan?

Under an option reload plan when an executive exercises an option and "pays" for the option with already-owned stock the executive will receive new options at the current market price for the same number of shares that were used to exercise the original option. If the executive chooses to exercise an option by paying cash, that executive does not receive the new options.

**Example:** On July 1, 1986, Executive C receives an option for 100 shares of Miller corporation stock with an option price of $25. On January 31, 1992, the current market price has risen to $45 and C exercises her option. To pay the exercise price, C surrenders already-owned shares sufficient to cover the $2,500 exercise price (at a market value of $45 per share, 56 shares would be required to cover the exercise). After tendering her option certificates and the 56 shares to Miller, C receives 100 shares of stock from the option exercise and, in addition, also receives a new option for 56 shares with an exercise price at the then current market price of $45. C now has 100 shares of stock valued at $45 per share (for which she paid $25 per share) and an option for an additional 56 shares at an exercise price of $45.

An option reload plan may be used in connection with both statutory and nonstatutory plans. Where this is the case, the reload option would be statutory if the option exercised was statutory, and nonstatutory if the option exercised was nonstatutory.

### Q. 6:37   In what situations does the use of an option reload feature make sense?

A reload feature makes sense for virtually all companies with stock option plans (although see Question 6:40 below for a caveat where ISOs are involved). Although allowing an executive to pay an option exercise price with already-owned shares allows him to end up with a larger number of shares after the exercise, he does not end up with the ownership level that the company wished to give him. Adding an option reload feature rectifies this situation.

**Planning Tip:** As an additional method to encourage stock retention after the reload, the reload plan could include a requirement that the shares received upon the exercise of the original option be held for a certain period in order for the reload option to vest.

### Q. 6:38   What is the accounting impact of a reload option?

The Financial Accounting Standards Board (FASB) has taken the position that there will be no accounting charge to the company as long as the exercise price of the reload option and the price of the original option is the market value at the time of grant, the term of the reload option does not extend past the term of the original option, and the total number of shares issuable does not exceed the number of original option shares.

### Q. 6:39   What is the tax treatment of a reload option?

The tax consequences of the reload option would be the normal tax consequences of statutory or nonstatutory options, depending on the type of option the reload option is deemed to be.

### Q. 6:40   Are there any special restrictions on the granting of reload options?

A company must be very careful in granting a reload option in connection with the exercise of an ISO because if the ISO did not contemplate the granting of a reload option at the time of grant, the reload feature will modify the terms of the ISO, thereby disqualifying it for preferred tax treatment.

Other than that, the only restrictions on the granting of reload options result from the requirements set forth by the FASB for avoiding the accounting charge. If any of these conditions are not met, then the company must recognize expense as it would in the case of a variable plan, such as that applicable to SAR plans, which would significantly detract from the attractiveness of the mechanism.

### Q. 6:41   What is a restricted stock purchase plan?

A restricted stock purchase plan is a plan under which an executive purchases shares of the company at their fair market value or at a discount from their fair market value. The stock is subject to forfeiture unless certain conditions are met. The company may also choose to make an outright grant of the restricted stock or to effectively make an outright grant by setting the purchase price of the stock at its nominal or par value (see Chapter 7).

### Q. 6:42   What are some of the restrictions which can be put on restricted stock?

Restricted stock can be subject to many different conditions to fulfill many company goals, including a condition of continued employment and the meeting of certain performance goals by the executive, his department or the company. Restrictions can cover periods after the termination of the executive's employment, and be drafted to provide for forfeiture of the stock if the executive attempts to steal clients or employees of the company or otherwise attempts to harm the company. In certain cases, these restrictions will constitute a substantial risk of forfeiture while in others, they will not.

If the shares are subject to forfeit if the executive is fired for cause or because he has committed a crime, or he accepts a job with a competing firm, these are not restrictions that will create a substantial risk of forfeiture. However, conditioning the vesting of the stock on the future performance of substantial services or on the occurrence of a future event (such as achieving performance goals) will create a substantial risk of forfeiture. [Treas Reg § 1.8303(c)(1) and (2)]

In most cases, the company will want to tie the executive to the company, and will therefore impose a service requirement. However, a few companies will decide to have the stock forfeited only if the executive takes a job with a competitor. They justify this decision by the immediate tax deduction available to them, and by the rationale that the restriction gets them the "important" part of the service requirement.

### Q. 6:43   How prevalent are restricted stock purchase plans?

Restricted stock purchase plans are used infrequently and when they are used they tend to be utilized by privately-held companies that offer restricted stock to nonowner-executives. In most cases, however, companies seem to prefer to make outright grants of restricted stock or, at the very least, to set the purchase price at the par value of the stock. (This much more common long-term incentive is discussed more in detail in Chapter 7.)

### Q. 6:44   What is the accounting treatment of a restricted stock purchase plan?

While under the tax rules the tax event can be postponed if the executive's interest in the restricted stock is subject to a substantial risk of forfeiture, this deferral is not available from an accounting point of view. Instead, a corporation will have to reflect an immediate compensation cost in the amount, if any, by which the market price of the stock exceeds the amount actually paid for the stock by the employee.

If a service requirement is a condition for the vesting of the restricted stock, then the amount of the compensation expense is accrued and charged against earnings over the applicable service period. The appreciation in the value of the shares from the date of grant to the date of vesting is not recognized as a compensation expense even though the full value of the shares at vesting may be deductible by the corporation, unless the vesting is based on performance, in which case the full value of the restricted stock, as appreciated, must be ratably charged against earnings.

### Q. 6:45  What is the tax treatment of a restricted stock purchase plan?

As long as restricted stock is subject to a substantial risk of forfeiture, the initial tax event for both the company and the executive will be deferred until the restrictions lapse. At that time, the executive realizes income, subject to the applicable withholding requirements, for which the company receives a corresponding compensation deduction, in the amount of the then fair market value of the stock. However, if the executive files a Code Section 83(b) election, he realizes income on the date of grant equal to the then-current fair market value of the stock, with a corresponding compensation deduction for the corporation.

If an executive has filed a Code Section 83(b) election, dividends received on restricted stock are dividend income and not deductible by the corporation. If the executive has not filed a Code Section 83(b) election, those dividends are compensation income subject to the applicable withholding requirements, and the corporation may deduct the amount of dividends paid as a compensation expense as long as the stock remains subject to a substantial risk of forfeiture. Similarly, if the stock were not subject to a substantial risk of forfeiture upon grant, the company would deduct the value of the stock in the year it is transferred to the executive (and lose the later ability to deduct dividend payments). However, the executive would be taxed on receipt of the stock and would not be entitled to a deduction for any loss if he subsequently forfeited the stock.

### Q. 6:46  What are the advantages of a restricted stock purchase plan?

A restricted stock purchase plan is an attractive compensation technique that fulfills the company's goals of turning its executives into stockholders. The restrictions on transferability operate as a form of handcuffs that are necessary to retain key individuals within the company. It also allows the company to provide an immediate benefit to its executives who, as holders of restricted stock, are entitled to dividends on their stock even though those shares may be subject to forfeiture.

When granted to an executive at full value in lieu of a bonus that would otherwise be paid in cash, restricted stock defers the tax event until the lapse of the restrictions.

### Q. 6:47  What are the disadvantages of a restricted stock purchase plan?

To the extent that the purchase requires a significant investment by the executive, that investment is a disadvantage because the interest on any debt incurred is not deductible. However, from a shareholder's perspective, the executive still benefits because even if the price of the stock remains constant or slightly decreases that executive will still realize gain due to the discounted price of the stock.

### Q. 6:48  What is the earnings per share impact of a restricted stock purchase plan?

For purposes of computing both the primary and full diluted earnings per share, the restricted shares should be treated as outstanding shares. As a result, earnings per share are affected not only as a result of the compensation expense but also as a result of the additional number of outstanding shares.

### Q. 6:49  For what type of a company does a restricted stock purchase plan make sense?

Restricted stock purchase plans are appropriate for companies that do not want to expand the number of shareholders that are not employees of the company and the tenure restrictions appeal to those companies that are concerned with executive turnover.

### Q. 6:50  What is a book value plan?

A book value plan is essentially a restricted stock purchase plan that awards shares of stock to the executive at a purchase price equal to the stock's book value and subject to the condition that the executive must resell the shares to the company upon the termination of employment at a price equal to the book value of the shares of stock at the time of termination. During the period the executive owns the stock, he or she is entitled to full voting and dividend rights in the stock.

> **Example:** On July 1, 1985, Executive D was granted the right to purchase 2,000 shares of stock from her employer Gable corporation at a price equal to the current book value of $42. D exercises this right by paying Gable $84,000. At the time of the exercise the book value of the shares was $45. On January 19, 1991, D retires and is required to resell the shares to the company. At this time the book value of the shares is $65. D would realize a gain of $46,000, which is computed as follows:
>
> | | |
> |---|---|
> | Sale price | $130,000 ($65 × 2,000) |
> | Basis or purchase price | ( 84,000) |
> | Gain | 46,000 |

As an alternative arrangement, the repurchase price of the stock can be based on a multiple of the company's earnings over the period the book value shares were held. In that case, the executive would be given stock without dividend rights because the payment of dividends by the company does not reduce the eventual repurchase price.

In reality, a book value plan is very similar in concept to a phantom stock plan based on book value in that the executive receives the appreciation in a company's book value over the period of time the shares are owned. However, the tax treatment for the two methods is different and must be considered. (See Chapter 7 for further discussion of phantom stock arrangements.)

### Q. 6:51   What is the tax treatment for a book value plan?

The tax treatment for a book value plan is the same as that for a restricted stock purchase plan. However, because the book value of the stock is not being sold at a discount to the executive, there is no tax event at the time of grant to either the company or the executive. When the company repurchases the stock from the executive it is not entitled to a deduction for the "loss" it has incurred by selling shares at a lower price than that at which it repurchases them, nor for the conceptual compensatory element resulting from the increase in the value of the shares. On the other hand, the appreciation that the executive receives is taxed as a capital gain.

### Q. 6:52   What are the advantages of a book value plan?

Many publicly-traded companies feel that compensating the executive on the actual increase in the company's book value rather than as a result of the vagaries of the stock market constitutes the primary advantage of book value plans and privately-held companies benefit from not having to perform costly and often inaccurate appraisals (see Q. 6:54).

### Q. 6:53   What are the disadvantages of a book value plan?

From the company's perspective, a book value plan achieves much the same compensatory goal as a phantom stock arrangement, yet is less advantageous from a tax point of view because the company is neither entitled to a deduction at the time of grant nor to any deduction, either for compensation or for a loss, at the time it repurchases the shares.

From the executive's perspective, while he or she is not penalized if the stock market value of the stock declines despite an increase in the company's book value, that executive will receive no benefit from a potentially inflated price-earnings ratio as reflected in the stock market value of the shares.

### Q. 6:54   For what type of companies does a book value plan make sense?

Book value plans are helpful to a privately-held company whose stock does not have an easily ascertainable market value, but wants to achieve the goals usually associated with stock-based plans. Although valuation of the stock can be obtained through the use of a professional appraiser, such a procedure involves additional expense to the company, and the results of the appraisal may not satisfy either the company or the executive.

A publicly-traded company can benefit from a book value plan in that it can give an equity interest in the company to its executives yet tie their reward to the company's performance rather than the vagaries of the stock market.

Many companies use a separate, nonvoting class of stock for use in their book value plans, and those who base the repurchase price on a multiple of earnings use a nondividend class of stock for their book value plans. These approaches would, however, not be appropriate for an S corporation because of the one-class-of-stock restriction.

### Q. 6:55  What is a convertible debenture?

A convertible debenture is a fixed income debt security that is sold at a fixed price to an employee. The debenture has a face value on which periodic interest is paid to the executive and it is typically convertible into stock of the company at a later date such as after the executive has completed a specified period of employment or specific performance goals has been met. Most companies have traditionally included a provision in the plan that the conversion right will be terminated if the debenture is transferred in order to discourage executives from transferring the debentures.

Convertible debentures involve securities that have to be registered under federal and most state laws unless an available exemption exists and the availability of an exemption depends on the details of each offer or offering.

**Example:** On February 3, 1985, Kristina purchased a convertible debenture from Altoona corporation that had a ten-year maturity, a face value of $10,000 and paid an annualized interest rate of 8 percent. The current market value of the stock was $25. The debenture allowed a conversion to Altoona stock if, after five years, Kristina was still employed and the return on investment (ROI) over the five-year period was at least 9 percent. The conversion ratio was 40 shares for each $1,000 face value of the debenture equivalent to a purchase price of $25 per share. Each year, Kristina was to receive $800 interest on the debenture, which would be taxable income to Kristina and deductible to the Altoona corporation.

In March 1990, the Altoona corporation achieved or exceeded its 9 percent target rate of return and Kristina was still an executive with the company. Kristina's debenture, therefore, became convertible to 400 shares of stock. Kristina elected to convert the debentures at the point when the market value of the stock was $36 per share. At the time of this conversion, neither Kristina nor the company experienced any tax consequences.

In April 1991, Kristina decided to sell her 400 shares of stock for the then-current market price of $39 per share. She had a gain of $5,600, which is computed as follows:

| | |
|---|---|
| Proceeds from sale | $15,600  ($39 × 400 shares) |
| Purchase price or basis | (10,000) |
| Gain | 5,600 |

The sale of the stock has no impact on the company.

### Q. 6:56 Is shareholder approval required to issue convertible debentures?

Although shareholder approval is not generally required to issue convertible debentures, approval of the Board of Directors is required when a company issues a debt obligation. However, it is prudent to obtain shareholder approval to avoid the possibility of a shareholder lawsuit challenging the appropriateness of the debt issuance.

### Q. 6:57 What is the accounting impact of a convertible debenture?

To the extent that the debentures are sold at more than full market value there would be no expense or other liability for accounting purposes.

### Q. 6:58 What is the tax treatment for a convertible debenture?

If the convertible debenture is purchased by the employee at its fair market value, no tax event occurs at that time. If the market value of the debenture is greater than the amount paid by the executive, then that excess is included in the executive's income, and deducted by the corporation as a compensation expense, in the year of purchase. There is no taxable event to the company or the employee when the debenture is converted, however, upon the sale of the underlying shares, the employee is taxed on the gain he or she is deemed to have incurred, which is the sale price of the shares less the amount he or she paid for the converted debenture.

Interest paid on the debenture prior to its conversion will be interest income to the executive and an interest deduction to the company. (For an example of how a convertible debenture works see Q. 6:55.)

### Q. 6:59   What is the earnings per share impact of a convertible debenture?

If the debenture's cash yield at the date of issuance is two-thirds of the bank prime interest rate, then the debentures are treated as common stock cash equivalents. As a result, earnings per share are affected not only as a result of the compensation expense but also as a result of the additional number of outstanding shares.

### Q. 6:60   What are the advantages of a convertible debenture program?

The principal advantages of using a convertible debenture is that the executive invests money in the company, which closely ties the interests of the executive and the shareholders. A convertible debenture program also minimizes the executive's downside risk by providing a fixed obligation of the company to pay both principal and interest to the executive and, if the stock price declines, the executive would still receive his or her principal back at the time the debenture matures. Furthermore, because interest at the prevailing interest rate is typically paid on the amount invested in the debenture, if the executive chooses not to convert, that executive will get his or her money back with interest, so the executive does not suffer a lost opportunity cost.

### Q. 6:61    What are the disadvantages of a convertible debenture program?

The primary disadvantage of a convertible debenture is that in most states it has to be registered under both federal and state securities laws, and the time and expense involved in this process may make the program prohibitive. Another disadvantage is the lack of executive involvement in the company stock's down side. Finally, the requirement that the executive make a substantial capital investment in order to participate in the program may be a problem because interest on any debt used to finance the purchase of the debenture is not deductible to the executive.

### Q. 6:62    For what type of company does a convertible debenture plan make sense?

A convertible debenture plan makes sense for those companies whose compensation philosophy includes the belief that an executive should make a substantial investment in the company's future, but who also recognize that because of the substantial investment required of the executive, his or her participation in the company stock's down side should be minimized.

### Q. 6:63    What is a junior stock plan?

"Junior stock" is a class of stock having lesser voting, dividend and liquidation rights, than ordinary common stock. Under a junior common stock plan, an executive receives junior stock that becomes convertible at a favorable rate into common stock. Junior stock plans were popular until the SEC and FASB proposed a rule that would require the full spread at conversion to be treated as an expense item to be reflected in the profit and loss statement and chargeable against earnings. This change eliminated the effectiveness of junior common stock and most organizations dropped their existing plans.

**Example:** Executive E is an executive of Altoona corporation. On January 1, 1988, he was granted and exercised an option to acquire 1,000 shares of Altoona's junior common stock at $1 per share. The junior stock converts to common stock if earnings per share reaches $12 by December 31, 1991. The current market value of Altoona corporation shares is $10. On January 1, 1992, Altoona

Corporation's earnings per share is $14 and E is still an executive with the company. Therefore, the junior common stock converts to regular common stock.

### Q. 6:64   What are the advantages of a junior stock plan?

The primary advantage of a junior stock plan, prior to the SEC and FASB changes, was that it provided the executive with capital gains treatment not only on the future growth in value of the common stock, but also on the initial spread between the acquisition cost of the junior common stock and the common stock value at the date of purchase of the junior common stock. This offered substantial leverage in providing low cost equity participation to executives. Tax reform changes coupled with the SEC and FASB rulings have stripped junior stock plans of these advantages.

### Q. 6:65   What are the disadvantages of a junior stock plan?

In addition to the lack of tax deductibility, three disadvantages of junior stock result from its use of a separate class of stock. First, the device is unavailable to the S corporation. Second, shareholder approval is likely to be required in order to authorize the new class of stock, unless such a class already exists. Lastly, the value to public companies of a second class of stock that would in all likelihood not be registered is limited, as the executive's ability to resell their shares is limited.

### Q. 6:66   How prevalent are junior common stock plans?

Junior stock plans have been adopted by many high technology companies and other companies that anticipated high stock price appreciation. Since FASB ruled that a charge to earning is required at the time of exchange, these plans have all but disappeared.

# Chapter 7

# Appreciation and Full-Value Plans

Appreciation and full-value plans are forms of long-term incentive plans that provide the executive with a benefit interest that, unlike purchase plans, does not require any actual investment. The most common type of appreciation plan is the stock appreciation right (SAR) plan while the two most common types of full-value plans are restricted stock grants (RSGs) and performance unit plans (PUPs). This chapter addresses the tax, legal and financial implications of appreciation and full-value plans, including the circumstance where these types of plans work best and their relative strengths and weaknesses.

## Q. 7:1 What are appreciation plans?

Appreciation plans are capital accumulation plans that grant the executive the right to receive the value of stock appreciation. Appreciation is most typically based on changes in the fair market value of the stock. Another approach is to measure the appreciation based on appreciation of the book value of the company. These plans do not require the executive to make an investment.

## Q. 7:2 What are examples of appreciation plans?

The most prevalent type of appreciation plan is the stock appreciation rights plan (SAR).

## Q. 7:3   What is a stock appreciation right?

A stock appreciation right (SAR) is the right to receive the value of the appreciation of a specified number of shares of a company's capital stock over a specified period of time. An SAR plan can provide that an SAR be exercised by the employee or may specify a maturity date. At exercise or maturity, the executive will receive a payment equal to the appreciated value of the underlying shares. The appreciation may be paid in any combination of cash, stock or other consideration, as specified in the SAR, although the combination payment usually attempts to pay enough cash to meet the executive's tax liability.

The appreciation measured by an SAR is usually the appreciation in a stock's market price because the SAR is usually used by public companies. However, the SAR can be linked to appreciation in earnings, book value or some other measure. SARs may be issued alone or linked with other compensation devices—usually stock options. SARs that are granted in tandem with stock options utilize one of two approaches. In tandem stock option/SAR plans, the exercise of the SAR or the stock option cancels the other compensation device. In non-tandem plans, both the option and the SAR are exercised separately and the executive receives an award from both.

**Example:** Anne is an executive with Altoona corporation. She participates in Altoona corporation's long-term incentive plan, which grants SARs and nonqualified stock options (NQSOs). On January 1, 1986, Anne is granted a nonqualified option for 1,000 shares and a SAR covering 10,000. The option price and the base price of the SAR is $20 per share, which represents the current market price of the stock. There is a one-year vesting and the plan life is ten years. During the "window period" in 1988, Anne exercises her option as to 500 shares and her SAR as to 2,500 shares. The current market value of a share is $26.

|                    | Option     | SAR      |
|--------------------|-----------|----------|
| Fair Market Value  | $13,000   | $15,000  |
| Amount Paid        | (10,000)  | (    0)  |
| Taxable Income     | 3,000     | 15,000   |
| Tax @ 28 percent   | (   840)  | ( 4,200) |
| NET                | $ 2,160   | $10,800  |

The effect of the exercise on Kristina's cash flow would be as follows:

| | |
|---|---:|
| Cash needed for the option | $10,000 |
| Cash needed for tax on option | 840 |
| Cash needed for tax on SAR | 4,200 |
| TOTAL CASH NEEDED | 15,040 |
| Cash received from SAR | (15,000) |
| NET CASH NEEDED | $    40 |

### Q. 7:4  How do the Section 16 rules affect stock appreciation rights?

If rewards are payable in stock, then even if the reward is actually paid in cash, the SAR is considered to be a derivative security, subject to Section 16(a) reporting requirements and Section 16(b) liability. Therefore, the SAR plan should take care to comply with the applicable Rule 16b-3 plan provisions, the most significant of which is shareholder approval in order to ensure that the grant of SARs will be an exempt transaction. Even if rewards are payable only in cash, the grant of an SAR will not be exempt from Section 16 unless it complies with the 16b-3 plan rules discussed in Chapter 6 in relation to stock option plans. Furthermore, the SAR must be held for six months before it is exercised, and unless that exercise is automatic or is fixed under the plan on a date more than six months after its date of grant and outside the holder's control, may be exercised only during a ten-day "window period" that begins on the third business day after the company releases its annual or quarterly financial information. Failure to comply with these requirements turns the exercise of the SAR into a sale of the underlying shares for purposes of Section 16.

### Q. 7:5  How prevalent are stock appreciation rights?

The most prevalent use of SARs is in conjunction with a stock option plan. Approximately 60 percent of large publicly traded companies utilize this capital accumulation vehicle, although this is expected to decrease dramatically.

### Q. 7:6   What is the accounting impact of an SAR Plan?

An SAR is considered to be a "variable plan award" in accounting terminology, that is, the number of shares of stock to be granted to or purchased by an executive or the price of such shares is not determinable until after the actual grant. When it grants an SAR, a company must measure compensation as the amount by which the value of the shares covered by the SAR exceeds the option price or value specified. Changes in the market value of the shares between the date of grant and the measurement date result in a change in the measure of the compensation. The measurement date is the date on which both the number of shares the executive is entitled to receive and the exercise or purchase price, if any, is known. [FASB Interpretation No 28 (AC Section 4062-1)]

The potential compensation expense will therefore fluctuate with the value of the company's stock, yet the company cannot wait until the final compensation amount is established because accounting rules require that the compensation be accrued as a charge to expense over the related period or periods the employee performs the related services. The compensation expense is accrued proportionately over the service period with adjustments to reflect the increases or decreases in the value of the shares.

Earnings per share are affected each period as a result of the additional compensation expense. If the SAR reward is to be paid in shares of common stock, they are deemed to be common stock equivalents and earnings per share will be further affected as a result of the larger number of shares deemed to be outstanding.

### Q. 7:7   What is the tax treatment for a stock appreciation rights plan?

There is no taxation upon the grant of an SAR. The holder of an SAR recognizes income only when the SAR matures or is exercised in an amount equal to the consideration received upon the maturity or exercise of the SAR. However, the IRS has ruled that if the SAR imposes a limit on the consideration that can be received by the executive upon exercise or maturity, the executive realizes the income when that maximum has been obtained whether or not the SAR is then matured or exercised unless the SAR is linked to a stock option.

From the company's point of view, if the SAR is exercised for cash, the company is entitled to a compensation deduction upon the exercise or maturity of the SAR. If the SAR is exercised for stock, the company is entitled to deduct as a business expense the amount of income recognized by the executive. Note that in this case the rules applying to transfers of stock made in connection with the performance of services (that is, the provisions of Code Section 162 that requires compensation to be reasonable) are applicable.

Finally, any SAR payments, whether in cash or in stock, are subject to withholding.

### Q. 7:8   When do stock appreciation rights typically vest?

Typically, the vesting of a SAR granted with a stock option will mirror the vesting of the stock option to which it is attached, which is a requirement in the case of ISOs. The exercise time period will also mirror that of the option.

### Q. 7:9   What are the advantages of a stock appreciation rights plan?

For the executive, SARs provide the holder with a cashless way of receiving the benefits of the appreciation in the company's stock although the gain itself is the same as afforded by a stock option.

The primary advantages of using an SAR resulted from the Section 16 rules. Under the prior Section 16 rules, SARs provided a way to ensure that an insider would have the cash necessary to exercise the options because he or she could not raise the money by selling company stock within six months of that exercise. Using an SAR also allowed the executive to effectively lock in his gain on the option shares. However, with the recent revision of the Section 16 rules these advantages are lost.

One of the remaining uses of SARs is to provide a benefit to partly "bail out" an underwater stock option, which is an option whose exercise price is higher than the market value for the stock. To do this, the company grants a non-tandem SAR whose base price is set at the then current (lower) market price, and this has the effect of reducing the effective option exercise price.

**Example:** Assume that Company A had granted a stock option to an executive with an exercise price of $30 per share and the market price of the stock has since fallen to $20. The company could grant an SAR to the executive with a base price of $20. If the price of the stock then rises to $40, the executive can exercise the SAR and the option at the same time for a $20 profit.

### Q. 7:10   Are there disadvantages to using stock appreciation rights?

Yes. The primary disadvantage of an SAR plan is its negative accounting consequence, which is that the company must take a charge to its earnings during each period in which an SAR is outstanding.

SARs are also very costly to the company. Although an SAR provides the same net benefit to the executive as a stock option plan, with a stock option the appreciation is "free" to the company and it receives money from the executive as well. With an SAR, the company must pay the appreciation itself. Finally, SARs do not fulfill the general goal of encouraging stock ownership by executives. Nor do they provide voting, dividend or other rights associated with stock ownership.

### Q. 7:11   For what type of company does a stock appreciation rights plan make sense?

Many public companies had SAR plans but limited participation in those plans to insiders. Now that the Section 16 advantage of a SAR is gone there is virtually no type of company for which an SAR plan makes sense because of the remaining negative tax and accounting consequences.

### Q. 7:12   What are full-value plans?

Full-value plans are capital accumulation plans that grant the executive the full value of a company's stock. As in appreciation plans, the value can be either the fair market value of the stock or the value can be based on a formula. The most typical formula approach is a book value formula where the executive receives the value of the stock at the time of the grant plus the appreciation over a specified period of time. Note that full value plans do not require the executive to make an investment.

## Q. 7:13  Why would a company choose to implement a full-value plan rather than a purchase plan?

Whether a company believes that an executive should make an investment in the company will often determine which type of plan it chooses to implement. Both full value and purchase plans permit the executive to gain from the appreciation in the price of a company's stock. However, a full value plan gives the executive the value of the underlying stock while the purchase plan requires the executive to actually purchase the value of the underlying stock.

## Q. 7:14  What is a phantom stock plan?

A phantom stock plan is a plan in which executives are granted "pretend" (or "phantom") shares of stock rather than real shares. Phantom stock is a right to a bonus based on the performance of "phantom" (rather than real) shares of a corporation's common stock over a specified period of time. The bonus is typically an amount equal to the difference between the fair market value of the shares of common stock on the date of grant and the fair market value of the stock at the later specified date, although the difference can be measured using book value or some other performance measure. Phantom stock plans are similar to stock appreciation right (SAR) plans, except that participants often have no choice with respect to the specified date of exercise in the typical phantom stock plan. The award when the phantom stock is converted may be paid out in either cash or stock.

**Example:** Kristina is an executive with Gable corporation. On August 28, 1986, Kristina is granted 1,000 shares of phantom stock that has a book value at the time of grant of $10 per share. The plan will vest in five years. During the five years the Gable corporation declares an 8 percent dividend. The plan credits additional shares to Kristina's account for the dividend payments as follows:

| Year | Book Value | Beginning Year | Additions From Dividends | End of Year |
|------|-----------|----------------|--------------------------|-------------|
| 1986 | $10       | $1,000         | $ 80                     | $1,080      |
| 1987 | 10.60     | 1,080          | 86.40                    | 1,166.40    |
| 1988 | 11.30     | 1,166.40       | 93.31                    | 1,259.71    |
| 1989 | 12        | 1.259.71       | 100.77                   | 1,360.48    |
| 1990 | 12.80     | 1,360.48       | 108.84                   | 1,469.32    |
| 1991 | 13.60     | 1,469.32       | 117.55                   | 1,586.87    |

On August 29, 1991, Kristina is credited with 1,586.87 shares. The appreciation value from the initial date of grant is $3.60 and Kristina receives $5,712.73. Gable corporation is entitled to a deduction of $5,712.73, which represents that amount that Kristina reports as taxable income.

A phantom stock plan, like an SAR plan, is subject to Section 16(a) reporting and Section 16(b) liability if rewards are payable in stock (even if the rewards are in fact paid in cash), and should therefore fully comply with the Rule 16b-3 provisions so that grants under the plan will be exempt transactions. However, even if rewards are payable only in cash, the phantom stock will be deemed to be a derivative security and treated like an option for purposes of the Section 16 rules, if its value is "derived from the value of an equity security." If the value of the phantom stock is determined from a formula based on earnings per share and return on equity, it will be a derivative security because it derives its value from the components of an equity security.

From the company's perspective, the use of phantom stock achieves the goals of increasing the executive's economic interest in the company and permitting him to participate in its growth, and yet permits the existing shareholders to retain all voting and liquidation rights associated with their ownership of shares. From the executive's perspective, he or she can acquire these interests without laying out funds or being subject to an immediate tax.

Phantom stock plans are sometimes utilized as a mechanism for a deferred compensation arrangement. Under this scenario, the executive elects to have his deferred compensation expressed in phantom shares of a company's stock. This sort of phantom stock plan is discussed more in depth in Chapter 9.

### Q. 7:15  Are dividends paid on phantom stock?

Dividends may but need not be paid on phantom stock. Some companies choose to pay dividends based on the philosophy that they have provided the executive with an interest which mirrors the interest of a shareholder. Other companies focus on the increased compensation expense that they must recognize for financial accounting purposes and choose not to pay or accrue phantom dividends.

Dividends may either be accrued or actually paid on phantom stock. If dividends are to be paid out, they result in income to the executive without deduction to the corporation. If dividends are accrued, they may be either allocated to the executive and eventually paid out when the phantom stock is paid out, or they may be converted into phantom stock themselves. This latter method results in a compounding of the benefit, and provides a far greater benefit from holding phantom stock than actual shares of stock.

### Q. 7:16  How prevalent are phantom stock plans?

Phantom stock plans are not used frequently by publicly-held corporations: fewer than 5 percent of public companies utilize this capital accumulation method for rewarding their executives. Private companies use this method much more frequently, although it is impossible to gather any statistics because of the absence of available public information.

### Q. 7:17  What is the accounting impact for a phantom stock plan?

Appreciation in the value of the units and any dividends paid or credited during the period is reported as a compensation expense to the company. A public company will accrue the expense and charge it against earnings on a quarterly basis.

Because no stock is actually issued, the only impact on earnings per share in any period is the amount of compensation expense recognized by the company for financial reporting purposes.

### Q. 7:18   What is the tax treatment for a phantom stock plan?

The executive has no income, and the corporation receives no tax deduction upon the grant of phantom stock units.

As long as the executive does not have the right to any distribution from his phantom stock, other than dividends payable on the stock, the executive will not be taxed on his phantom stock until the units are converted to actual cash or stock. Whether he receives cash or stock, the executive will be taxed at ordinary income rates as if he received personal service compensation. The company is entitled to a deduction for the amount it pays to the executive, including the value of the stock distributed, as and when the executive realizes income, even if that amount includes phantom dividends accrued on the phantom stock.

If the executive is entitled to draw upon his phantom stock units, he will be deemed to be in constructive receipt of the units and taxed immediately on their value. Therefore, the company should make sure that the units are not set apart for him or otherwise made available so that he may draw upon them.

Of course, any dividends that are actually paid on phantom stock are subject to current compensation income taxation; no income is recognized in the case of phantom dividends until the conversion date.

If the executive receives stock as a result of the conversion, the appreciation in those shares will be taxed as a capital gain at the time he sells the shares.

### Q. 7:19   What are the advantages of a phantom stock plan?

A phantom stock plan allows the executive to participate in the growth of the value of the company without actually making him a shareholder and diluting the value of issued stock.

The executive receives the same value as with a grant of stock, and yet is not required to make an investment, so that he is not at risk if the company's performance falters. Furthermore, he is able to defer being taxed on the benefit, which he could not avoid with a grant of stock. From the company's perspective, unless the granted stock is restricted, phantom stock may have more of a "tying" incentive as the executive receives no benefit unless he continues with the company.

### Q. 7:20  Are there disadvantages to a phantom stock plan?

Yes. The principal disadvantage is that the costs are fully chargeable for financial accounting purposes as expenses as and when accrued. For smaller companies, or companies in cyclical businesses, this may be especially troubling.

Phantom stock that is converted into cash can be a severe drain on the company's cash, and many companies may not have sufficient cash flow to meet this potentially large expense. Therefore many companies prefer to convert phantom shares into real shares of stock.

### Q. 7:21  When do phantom stock units typically vest?

The typical vesting period for phantom stock units is five years.

### Q. 7:22  For what type of company does a phantom stock plan make sense?

In a privately-held corporation, there is more of an incentive to use phantom stock rather than a true stock-based compensation technique in order to avoid dilution to current shareholders, as well as more of a reason to pay out phantom stock conversions in cash rather than in stock (although this may not apply to a cash-poor privately-held company!). Privately-held companies will prefer to use phantom stock plans based on the book value of the stock, which will generally be much more easily ascertainable than the market value for the same stock.

### Q. 7:23  What is a shadow stock plan?

A shadow stock plan is another name for a phantom stock plan (see Q. 7:3).

### Q. 7:24   What is a restricted stock grant?

Under a restricted stock grant (RSG), an executive is granted shares of stock that are subject to forfeiture unless certain conditions are met, or he is given the opportunity to purchase those shares for their nominal or par value. The shares become available to the executive as the restrictions lapse, usually on the completion of a period of employment or based on the performance of the company. The executive receives dividends and has full voting rights on his shares of restricted stock.

A restricted stock grant is very similar to a restricted stock purchase plan as described in Chapter 6, however, the difference between the two is one of price to the executive. The same considerations apply with respect to the restrictions to be placed on the stock.

**Example:** On January 1, 1988, William Parsons, an executive at Gable corporation, receives, at no cost, an award of 1,000 restricted shares of Gable corporation. The restrictions will lapse on January 1, 1993, as long as William is an employee of Gable corporation at that time. If he leaves the company prior to that time the shares revert back to Gable corporation. At the time of the award, the shares are worth $10 each and the $10,000 total cost must be amortized as a compensation expense over the five-year period. On January 1, 1993, William is still employed by Gable corporation and the restrictions lapse. At this time the shares are worth $18 each. Assuming that William had not made an 83(b) election, he would recognize $18,000 as income on January 1, 1993, and the Gable corporation will be entitled to the corresponding $18,000 tax deduction, even though this amount differs from the $10,000 compensation expense it had accrued on its books.

### Q. 7:25   How prevalent are restricted stock grants?

The volatility of the stock market makes restricted stock a popular capital accumulation device because the executive receives value even if the stock price falls without having to make any personal investment under this type of plan. As a result, approximately half of the large publicly-traded companies utilize restricted stock grants.

Privately-held companies that offer RSGs usually attach two conditions to the grant. The first condition is that the executive receives the stock after all restrictions lapse and the second condition mandates that company has the right of first refusal if and when the executive wants to dispose of the stock.

### Q. 7:26   What is the accounting impact of a restricted stock grant?

While under the tax rules the tax event can be postponed if the executive's interest in the restricted stock is subject to a substantial risk of forfeiture, this deferral is not available from an accounting point of view. Instead, a corporation will have to reflect an immediate compensation cost equal to the value of the stock granted (less any nominal value the executive is required to pay).

If a service requirement is a condition for the vesting of the restricted stock, then the amount of the compensation expense is accrued over the applicable service period. However, note that if the stock is forfeited, the compensation expense recorded in previous periods can be reversed to reflect the amount of the forfeiture. The appreciation in the value of the shares from the date of grant to the date of vesting is not recognized as a compensation expense for accounting purposes even though the full value of the shares at vesting is deductible by the company, unless the vesting is based on performance, in which case the full value of the restricted stock, as appreciated, must be ratably charged against earnings.

Earnings per share calculations and book value of the outstanding shares of the company's stock are diluted because additional shares have been issued but no payment (or only a nominal one) has been received by the company.

### Q. 7:27   What is the tax treatment for a restricted stock grant?

The value of restricted stock granted to the executive will be taxable to the executive and deductible by the company in the year in which it is no longer subject to a substantial risk of forfeiture (remember that stock can be deemed for tax purposes to be not subject to a substantial risk of forfeiture and nevertheless end up being forfeited by the executive).

As long as no Section 83(b) election has been filed, dividends paid on restricted stock prior to the time the executive's rights become substantially vested can be deducted by the company as a compensation expense.

### Q. 7:28   How does a Section 83(b) election affect a restricted stock grant?

If an executive makes an 83(b) election on a grant or restricted stock, he will be taxed immediately on the fair market value of the restricted stock at the time of grant. Dividends paid on the shares will be normal dividend income to the executive, which is not subject to withholding and not deductible by the company. In the event that the executive elects 83(b) treatment and he later forfeits the subject stock, he will not be entitled to any refund for the taxes paid; he will, however, be entitled to treat the forfeiture as a sale of the stock at a loss.

### Q. 7:29   What is the typical vesting period for a restricted stock grant?

Restrictions on RSGs generally lapse in three to five years. Restrictions may lapse all at once at the end of the vesting period or in annual installments during the vesting period

### Q. 7:30   What are the advantages of a restricted stock grant?

A restricted stock grant program is attractive from the company's perspective, fulfilling the goals of turning management into stockholders, yet retaining them through the restrictions on transferability. Most companies believe that restricted stock is a strong motivation and retention mechanism for executives.

If restrictions are placed on the stock which do not give rise to a substantial risk of forfeiture, yet may result in the executive's forfeiting the shares in chosen events, the corporation is entitled to an immediate deduction for the stock. However, this will be seen as a disadvantage from the executive's perspective, as he will be subject to immediate tax on shares of stock that he runs the risk of losing.

### Q. 7:31   Are there disadvantages to a restricted stock grant?

Yes. Restricted stock is often criticized as a "freebie" for management because most companies condition the vesting of the stock only on service and do not impose any additional performance requirements. Therefore an executive will receive a reward even where there is no improvement in a company's performance, yet this is not the type of situation where a reward seems appropriate. Existing shareholders are diluted as a result of the grant of stock for which no purchase price—or only nominal one—has been paid.

### Q. 7:32   For what types of companies do restricted stock grants make sense?

Restricted stock may be most useful and defensible as grants to high potential middle managers and professional employees in order to recognize those individuals with unique skills and contributions who are not normally eligible to receive stock options. Furthermore, a company that has difficulties recruiting or retaining key contributors can use restricted stock grants as a recruitment bonus. Finally, restricted stock grants are especially attractive to private companies as the transfer restrictions ensure that outsiders will not be able to acquire shares of the company's stock.

### Q. 7:33   What is a performance unit plan?

A performance unit plan (PUP) grants the executive performance units based on company performance targets achieved over a specified period, generally between three to five years. The plan will set goals for the company, and establish the reward to be paid out if those goals are attained. The reward, which is the value of the performance unit, is generally set by a number of shares, but may be settled in cash or stock or a combination of both. As an interesting compensation twist, the payout from a performance unit plan may be made in restricted shares.

A performance unit plan that pays its reward in shares of restricted stock is similar to a restricted stock grant where the vesting of the shares is subject to a company performance standard. However, with a RSG, an executive receives the restricted shares immediately (even if he must return them later), and can receive dividends on those shares. He can also elect to be taxed immediately on the value at grant of those restricted shares.

Similarly, a performance unit plan that pays the reward in cash is similar to a phantom stock plan in that the executive is not entitled to the reward until the performance targets are met, yet the executive may be entitled to receive a reward under a performance unit plan even where the value of the shares has not increased.

A performance unit plan whose awards are payable in stock is of course subject to Section 16(a) reporting requirements and Section 16(b) liability. Even where awards are payable only in cash, the performance unit will be a derivative security if its value is derived from the value of an equity security. If more than 50 percent of the value of a performance unit is derived from factors unrelated to the value of the equity securities (examples include product quality, customer acceptance and interpersonal skills), a performance unit will not be deemed to be a derivative security. More guidance from the SEC is necessary on this issue.

### Q. 7:34   How does the performance standard work?

The company must determine the goals to be used for the plan, generally a growth in earnings per share, or in sales or profits, or improvement in profit margins, then the maximum payout if the highest target were reached. It must decide what compensation should be paid if those goals are met, if a lesser percentage of those goals are met, or if those goals are exceeded. The performance awards are generally determined on a group rather than on an individual basis, and the members of the group share in the reward relative to their contributions.

**Example:** Company A decides that it will allocate 100 shares of stock to a performance unit plan. It will pay out its maximum 100 share award if its profits grow by an average of 10 percent or more over the next three years, but will pay out 75 shares if profits grow by an average of 7.5 percent or more (but less than 10 percent) over the period, and 50 shares if profits grow by an average of 5 percent or more (but less than 7.5 percent) over the period. Company A has determined that it will make no awards if profits grow annually by less than 5 percent, and will pay out no "bonus" if profits grow by more than 10 percent. Assuming the 10 percent target is reached, the group of executives who participate in the Plan will share the 100 share award.

The performance unit plan may have more than one target outstanding at any one time, to cover different years.

### Q. 7:35  What is the accounting impact of a performance unit plan?

For financial accounting purposes, performance unit plans are treated as "variable plan awards" and thus subject to the same accounting treatment as stock appreciation rights (SARs). Therefore, the company will have to accrue the estimated compensation expense proportionately over the service/measurement period, with adjustments for any increases or decreases in market value.

Earnings per share are affected each period as a result of the additional compensation expense. In addition, if the performance unit plan contemplates payment of the award in shares of the company's stock, they are deemed to be common stock equivalents, and earnings per share will be further affected as a result of the larger number of shares deemed to be outstanding.

### Q. 7:36  What is the tax treatment for a performance unit plan?

The executive recognizes no income, and the company no deduction, at the time of grant of the performance units. Any increase during the performance period in the value of the shares that the executive may earn as a result of an award under the plan is not income to him. This is intuitively clear as the number of shares that will be awarded under a performance unit plan is not known at the time the goals are set because this will depend on what level of goal is met. Similarly, the value of the unit is unknown at the time of grant, even where the award is to be made in certain number of shares of stock, as the value of those shares at the later date is not then known.

The executive has income, and the company a deduction, upon the distribution of the performance units and the amount of income is the fair market value of the property received.

### Q. 7:37   What is the typical vesting period for a performance unit plan?

A typical performance unit plan vests in three to five years.

### Q. 7:38   What are the advantages of a performance unit plan?

The principal advantage of performance unit plans is that these plans provide a nonstock market related capital accumulation reward to executives in cases where stock market performance may not reflect corporate financial performance. Often these benefits are granted in tandem with stock options or other market based programs so that the executive is rewarded when the company achieves its objective even when the stock price doesn't perform well.

### Q. 7:39   Are there disadvantages to instituting a performance unit plan?

Yes. The primary disadvantage of performance unit plans is the difficulty in accurately establishing performance goals for three or more years in the future. Also, because these plans typically are payable at least partially in cash, a substantial charge to earnings may occur when goals are achieved. Finally, an important disadvantage of a performance unit plan is its negative accounting consequence. Specifically, the corporation must take a charge to its earnings during each measurement period of the plan.

### Q. 7:40   What is a performance share plan?

A performance share plan is a term often used interchangeably to mean a performance unit plan, although it generally refers to a performance unit plan that settles its awards entirely in shares of stock.

# Chapter 8

# Combination Long-Term Plans

Tandem plans are incentive plans that utilize more than one type of long-term incentive plan. Usually, tandem plans grant executives two types of options or awards and once the executive chooses one alternative the other is canceled. Two of the most common combination plans are the phantom stock/stock option plan and the restricted stock/stock option plan although a third variation of the tandem plan is the contingent stock award plan that requires the executive to purchase and hold one option before obtaining access to a second option or other award. This chapter covers the requirements for implementing tandem plans as well as how to maximize their effectiveness.

### Q. 8:1   What is a Tandem Plan?

A tandem plan grants an executive two types of capital accumulation plans and gives him or her the choice of receiving one or the other. By choosing or exercising one alternative, the other is canceled.

### Q. 8:2   Are there advantages to combining different forms of compensation or creating combination or tandem plans?

Yes. Combining nonqualified stock options with a capital accumulation vehicle that does not require an investment creates a very attractive plan for executives, because it grants the stock's appreciation potential through options while providing a "floor" benefit if the stock price does not go up.

### Q. 8:3 Are there disadvantages of combining different forms of compensation or creating tandem plans?

Yes. The prime criticism of the tandem plan is that these plans provide downside protection to the executive, which is a protection that the average shareholder does not receive.

### Q. 8:4 Which combinations of compensation are most common in tandem plans?

Three combinations are used most frequently. The combinations are:

- Phantom Stock and Stock Options (Tandem Phantom Stock/Stock Option);
- Restricted Stock and Stock Options; and
- Stock Appreciation Rights and Stock Options.

### Q. 8:5 What is a Tandem Phantom Stock/Stock Option Plan?

Although not very prevalent, a Tandem Phantom Stock/Stock Option Plan grants an executive fully vested phantom stock and a leveraged nonqualified stock option. These rights are, however, mutually exclusive. For example, cashing in the phantom units results in a forfeiture of the related option while the exercise of the option results in the cancellation of the related phantom units. The motivation for instituting a tandem phantom stock/stock option plan is that the executive receives the value of income to be deferred in phantom stock but at the same time also receives the opportunity to surrender the phantom stock for a more valuable option, if and when the appreciation of the option exceeds the value of the phantom stock.

**Example:** Bill is an executive at Gable corporation and is eligible to participate in the Gable Corporation Tandem Plan, which has a leverage ratio of 3 to 1 between the stock options and the phantom stock units. On December 31, 1986, William agrees to defer 50 percent of his 1987 annual incentive into the Gable

Corporation Tandem Plan. The fair market value of Gable stock in January, 1987 is $25 and on January 19, 1987, Bill is notified that his 1987 annual incentive plan payment is $100,000. As a result, Bill receives $50,000 in cash (less the appropriate tax) and, due to the 50 percent deferral, receives a $50,000 tandem grant of:

- 2,000 ($50,000/25) phantom stock units; and
- 6,000 nonqualified stock options at $25.

Assuming the plan has a deferral ratio of 3:1, if the stock price increases to $37.50, which is a 50% increase from the $25 option exercise price, exercising three options becomes as valuable as cashing in one unit of phantom stock. This is said to be the "cross-over" point. At a stock price of $37.75, the relationship between the stock and the options is:

|                | Phantom Stock | Non-Qualified Option |
|----------------|---------------|----------------------|
| Market Value   | $75,500       | $226,500             |
| Purchase Price | 0             | 150,000              |
| NET Value      | $75,500       | $ 76,500             |

In January, 1991, the stock price reaches a value of $48 and Bill exercises his options, which cancels his rights to the phantom stock and generates income as follows:

|                        |           |
|------------------------|-----------|
| Market Value           | $288,000  |
| Purchase price (basis) | (150,000) |
| Income                 | $133,000  |

### Q. 8:6  What is the accounting impact of a Tandem Phantom Stock/Stock Option Plan?

A compensation charge would be accrued at the time of grant in the amount of the grant. Any increases in the market price of the stock up to the crossover point would result in an additional compensation expense allocated to the phantom stock unit. (While isolated phantom stock units that are payable in cash would generally be subject to open-ended accounting charges, adding the stock option component creates an accounting ceiling for the units at the cross-over point).

At the time of the exercise, if the executive exercises as to the units, the phantom stock is treated as a compensation expense. On the other hand, if the options are exercised after the crossover point there is no accounting entry for the stock option component and any compensation expense charges that are related to the phantom stock portion are reversed.

### Q. 8:7 What is the tax treatment for a Tandem Phantom Stock/Stock Option Plan?

The executive recognizes no income on the grant of a tandem phantom stock/stock option and the company is unaffected by the grant as well because it receives a tax benefit only when the executive realizes taxable income.

Upon exercise, the executive has the right to exercise either the phantom stock or stock option alternative. If the phantom stock alternative is chosen, the current value of the stock is taxable to the executive as ordinary income. On the other hand, if the stock option is chosen, the executive is taxed on the spread in the value of the stock over the exercise price. In either case the company receives a compensation deduction that is equal to the amount on which the executive is taxed. Finally, the executive incurs additional income when he or she disposes of the stock acquired under a tandem phantom stock/stock option plan equal to the amount of appreciation that occurred since the time the option was exercised.

### Q. 8:8 Are there advantages to a Tandem Phantom Stock/Stock Option Plan?

Yes. The primary advantage to the executive is that he or she controls the distribution and tax timing of the compensation. Other advantages include the fact that the company can avoid any cash outflow if the phantom stock units are actually paid in stock while still tying the executive's compensation to the value of the company as measured by stock price. This is the case whether the executive chooses the phantom stock or the stock option. Furthermore, if this tandem plan is used as a deferred income mechanism, it totally protects the executive from a change of control problem because he or she can control the distribution. Finally, this type of plan helps to retain competent employees because the executive's phantom stock component is guaranteed only while the executive remains employed.

### Q. 8:9    Are there disadvantages to a Tandem Phantom Stock/Stock Option Plan?

Yes, because the phantom stock component requires an accounting charge, and if payable in cash, can be an expensive compensation mechanism for the company. If the executive chooses the stock option component, a significant disadvantage results because the executive must utilize his or her own cash to exercise option and this cash outlay often motivates an executive to sell rather than retain the company stock.

This type of tandem plan is also criticized for giving the executive a downside protection (in the form of phantom stock) for the stock option, which is a protection that shareholders do not have.

### Q. 8:10   For what type of company does a Tandem Phantom Stock/Stock Option Plan make sense?

A tandem phantom stock/stock option plan makes sense for a company that wants to give an executive an immediate financial stake in the company in the form of phantom stock but also permit the executive to benefit by way of the stock option component from any stock price appreciation that may result if the stock price increases substantially.

### Q. 8:11   What is a tandem restricted stock/stock option plan?

Although relatively new, a tandem restricted stock/stock option plan grants both restricted stock awards and nonqualified stock options. Under this type of plan the participant is allowed to choose whether to keep the restricted stock or to exercise the options, which cancels the restricted stock award. Furthermore, vesting of the restricted stock would also cancel the related stock option.

While this type of plan was initially designed to compensate outside members of the Board of Directors, it has been used in several instances as a capital accumulation plan for executives.

**Example:** David is an outside director of the Gable corporation, which provides its directors with an annual retainer fee of $36,000. One-half of the fee, or $18,000, is paid in cash and the remaining $18,000 is paid in to a Tandem Restricted Stock/Stock Option Plan at a ratio between the restricted stock and the stock options of 3 to 1. David receives 720 shares of restricted stock ($18,000/$25, the current market value) and 2,160 nonqualified stock options with an exercise price of $25. David receives annual dividends on the restricted stock until the restrictions lapse in 5 years at which point he will receive the stock and the corresponding nonqualified options will be canceled. In the alternative, David can exercise his options at any time before the restrictions lapse and forfeit the restricted stock.

The following table shows how much the stock price moves, therefore, determining whether the restricted stock or nonqualified stock option is a more advantageous alternative.

| Stock Price Appreciation (in %) | Value of 1 Restricted Share | Gain on 3 option shares above the exercise price | Excess Value of Options |
|---|---|---|---|
| 0 | $25.00 | 0.0 | $(25) |
| 20 | 30.00 | 15.0 | (15) |
| 30 | 32.50 | 22.50 | (10) |
| 40 | 35.00 | 30.00 | (5) |
| 50 | 37.50 | 37.50 | 0 |
| 60 | 40.00 | 45.00 | 5 |
| 70 | 42.50 | 52.50 | 10 |
| 80 | 45.00 | 60.00 | 15 |

Assuming a 3 to 1 ratio, the crossover point is at a 50 percent stock appreciation level. Above this point, David should exercise his options, which cancels the restricted stock ownership.

### Q. 8:12 What is the accounting impact of a Tandem Restricted Stock/Stock Option Plan?

A compensation expense earnings charge for the typical restricted stock grant would be incurred based upon the market value of the shares at grant and a variable award accounting charge would accrue over the service period. For a tandem grant the FASB would probably take the position that only the increases in the market price of the stock up to the crossover point (that is, where the appreciation of the options exceeds the appreciated value of the restricted stock) would result in a "variable award" accounting charge.

Up to the crossover point, the restricted stock award would be treated as other outstanding shares, therefore earnings per share would be affected each period as a result of that increased number of shares as well as by the compensation expense, which is recognized for financial reporting purposes. Above the cross-over point, the number of shares deemed to be outstanding would be determined in the same way as with stock options.

### Q. 8:13 What is the tax treatment for a Tandem Restricted Stock/Stock Option Plan?

The tax treatment at the time of grant would be similar to the tax treatment of two independent plans. That is, the executive would not recognize income on the restricted shares until they vested and the tax would be based on the market value at the time of vesting. As for the tandem nonqualified stock option, there would be no tax upon grant but when the executive chose to exercise the options he or she would be taxed and the company would be entitled to a tax deduction equal to the amount of the spread at the time of exercise. Finally, when the executive decides to dispose of the stock any appreciation that may have occurred since the exercise is taxed as ordinary income.

### Q. 8:14 What are the advantages of a tandem restricted stock/stock option plan?

This approach combines the advantages of both restricted stock and stock options to allow the executive to choose whether to retain the restricted stock or to exercise the stock option. As a result, ownership of the stock option ties the executive's reward to company performance as measured by stock price while the restricted stock component provides downside protection.

The primary advantage of this type of plan is that it gives executives and/or directors an immediate ownership position through the restricted stock so that the participant can vote and receive dividends but also take advantage of appreciation in the company's value by way of the nonqualified stock option.

## Q. 8:15   For what type of company does a tandem restricted stock/stock option plan make sense?

A company that wants to give immediate ownership to the executive, but still wants to require the executive to make an investment should consider a tandem restricted stock/stock option plan. Furthermore, a company that anticipates that its stock will appreciate above the crossover point can grant the executive an immediate stock ownership interest, but also guarantee that the executive will be rewarded for his or her financial investment.

## Q. 8:16   What are the disadvantages of the tandem restricted stock/stock option plan?

This type of plan is criticized because it offers downside protection through the restricted stock component that is not available to the average company shareholder. Furthermore, at a minimum, the executive will be rewarded for tenure, regardless of stock market performance and he or she need invest in the option plan only when the increase is sufficient to buy and sell so there is little motivation to hold the stock.

## Q. 8:17   What is a tandem stock appreciation right (SAR)/stock option Plan?

This type of tandem plan grants the executive stock appreciation rights in conjunction with nonqualified stock options and the executive may choose to receive either the SAR or the corresponding stock option. The real value of this type of tandem plan was the opportunity they offered insiders to raise the cash necessary to exercise their options and pay the required withholding amount without violating the 1934 Act, which precluded them from selling company shares within 6 months of the grant. Specifically, with this plan even insiders were allowed to essentially pay the option exercise price by using the increase in the value of the company shares, which decreased the amount of the personal investment the insiders were required to make. As a result they were put in a position that was comparable to an outsider who could simply pay the exercise price with the shares of already-owned stock.

Note that under the new Section 16 rules, if a cash-only SAR is granted in tandem with a stock option, the SAR becomes subject to the Section 16(a) reporting requirements and Section 16(b) liability as if it were payable in stock.

The SAR need not be granted at a base price equal to the exercise price of the option. Many companies set the base price of a tandem SAR higher than the exercise price of the related option to encourage the executive to exercise the option rather than the SAR.

Most companies grant one SAR for each option granted, although some prefer to grant a greater proportion of stock options than SARs.

**Example:** Anne is an executive of Altoona corporation and participates in their Long-Term Incentive Plan. On January 19, 1984, she receives 250 SARs with a $10 base price and an option for 1,000 nonqualified stock options with a $10 exercise price. The current market value of the stock is $10. On February 3, 1989, the current market value of Altoona stock has risen to $30. If Anne takes all the SARs she will receive $5,000 ($20 in appreciation × 250 SARs) and if she exercises all her options she will receive $20,000 [1,000 shares × ($30 current share price – $10.00 exercise price)].

### Q. 8:18   How prevalent are tandem SAR/stock option plans?

These plans historically have been the most common of the tandem plans with approximately 30 percent of all publicly-traded companies offering them to their executives. However, these plans are probably no longer necessary or even desirable because of the changes in the Section 16 rules. Under the new Section 16 rules, insiders can exercise their options and immediately sell the underlying securities without short-swing liability. Accordingly, the elimination of this potential liability should reduce the cash needs of insiders and eliminate the rationale associated with this type of plan.

### Q. 8:19   What is the accounting impact of a tandem SAR/stock option plan?

The accounting impact of the tandem SAR/stock option plan is a blending of the individual accounting consequences for each component. Although there is no accounting impact at the time of the grant of an option, the company is required to account for the SAR portion of the grant through proportionate charges to earning through the service period. On the exercise of the option or the SAR any excess charges can be reversed.

While a stand alone SAR is subject to open-ended accounting charges, adding the tandem option component creates a ceiling for the SAR at the cross-over point. Therefore, any increases in the market price of the stock up to the crossover point results in a compensation expense. Where the option is exercised above or after the crossover point, there is no accounting for the stock option component and any charges to compensation for the SAR are reversed.

### Q. 8:20   What is the tax treatment for a tandem SAR/stock option plan?

There is no tax impact to the company or to the executive at the time of the actual grant. The company receives a tax benefit in the form of a compensation deduction only when the executive receives and reports taxable income.

Upon exercise of the SAR, the executive will realize income and the company will receive a compensation deduction. The amount of income and the corresponding deduction equals the value of the cash or stock that the executive receives. If the option component is exercised, the executive will receive income, and the company will receive a corresponding deduction, equal to the amount of the spread. Finally, in the case of an SAR with a ceiling on the amount of appreciation that can be received by the executive, which become taxable income to the executive when the maximum is attained, the addition of a stock option will defer the tax event until the exercise of the SAR.

If the SAR is payable in stock, then under either the SAR or the stock option alternative the executive receives capital gains income equal to the appreciation that has occurred between the time of exercise and date of disposition.

# Chapter 9

# Income Deferral

Various tax reform measures have made significant cutbacks in the tax-favored treatment of employer-provided retirement benefits and perquisites. In response to the limitations of qualified plans, companies are implementing specialized executive programs to compensate for the regulatory limitations and respond to competitive recruiting pressures. Deferred compensation programs are playing an ever increasing role in the executive's total compensation package.

One approach to providing deferred compensation involves an agreement between the executive and the company for the executive to give up some portion of his or her current compensation in exchange for the company's promise to make a deferred payment sometime in the future. The second approach does not include any income deferral but involves an additional future payment that is provided by the company to the executive. This chapter covers the ERISA, IRA and general tax issues of deferred compensation as well as plan design and competitive practices.

## Income Deferral Overview

### Q. 9:1   What is deferred compensation?

Deferred compensation refers to the process of delaying receipt of income and its taxation to a later date through the use of a nonqualified compensation agreement that postpones payment of compensation until a later time, typically until after retirement.

### Q. 9:2  What are the two primary approaches for deferring compensation?

One approach involves an agreement between the executive and the company for the executive to give up some portion of his current compensation in exchange for the company's promise to make a deferred payment sometime in the future. Typically the executive defers some portion of his annual incentive plan. To encourage the executive to make this deferral, many companies offer a guaranteed investment return that is higher than the executive can hope to obtain on his own.

The second approach is for the company to provide an additional benefit to the executive. This second approach does not involve any income deferral on the part of the executive but does involve the company's promise to make additional payments to the executive at some time in the future.

Deferred compensation refers to either of these somewhat different approaches.

### Q. 9:3  What is a nonqualified deferred compensation plan?

A nonqualified deferred compensation plan is a plan that is not subject to most of the Internal Revenue Code (the Code). Because these plans are not subject to the Code they can be designed to cover selected executives and need not be available to the rank and file employees. The trade-off for this flexibility is that nonqualified benefit plans result in the recognition of income when the employee's right to the benefit vests rather than deferring recognition of the income to the time of the distribution as would be the case with a qualified plan.

### Q. 9:4   How does a nonqualified deferred compensation plan differ from a qualified plan?

Nonqualified plans do not qualify for the special tax treatment afforded to plans that meet the qualification requirements contained in Code Section 401(a). This favorable tax treatment for qualified plans includes a current deduction for the employer for its contributions, tax deferral for the employee on the contributions, and tax free build-up of investment income.

### Q. 9:5   What do nonqualified deferred compensation plans typically provide?

Because a nonqualified deferred compensation plan is usually tailored to one executive or a small group of executives these plans vary greatly in what they provide. Typically these plans provide for postretirement payments to the executive, postretirement and pre-retirement death benefits and preretirement disability payments. Some of the plans provide for payments prior to retirement. Except in the case of Section 457 plans there is no restriction on the amount to be deferred. And because a nonqualified plan is not attempting to satisfy IRS regulations the plan can be highly discriminatory as to who is covered and what benefits are provided.

### Q. 9:6   What is the rationale for creating nonqualified deferred compensation plans for executives?

The Tax Reform Act of 1986 (TRA '86) imposed a series of limitations on the benefit levels that highly paid executives can receive. Chief among these limitations were:

- Capping individual 401(k) contributions at $7,000. This figure is adjusted annually to reflect the movement of the consumer price index;
- Freezing the Section 415 limits on deferred compensation plans;
- Limiting to $200,000 the earnings that can be included in the calculations of qualified retirement plan benefits;
- Toughening the anti-discrimination testing for 401(k) plans and other benefits; and
- Levying a 15 percent excise tax on excess distributions from tax qualified retirement plans.

These reforms spurred many companies to develop alternative nonqualified deferred compensation plans that could be used to ensure that executives who were adversely impacted by these provisions would be made whole, especially at retirement.

### Q. 9:7 What are the typical objectives of the executive in deferring income under a nonqualified deferred compensation plan?

The executive who defers compensation is probably doing so in anticipation that the executive's future tax rate will be lower. Deferral of compensation is also a method of forced savings, much like a Christmas Club Savings account at a bank. It makes sense for a highly-paid employee, who is at the highest marginal tax rate to defer income if the executive feels that the marginal tax rate will be lower at some future time when the executive receives the deferred income.

### Q. 9:8 What are the typical objectives of the company in providing a deferral program?

The primary reasons for providing deferred compensation plans to executives is the need for companies to attract and retain executives. Competition for executives forces companies to try to develop compensation plans that will be attractive to executives and as qualified plans become more and more restricted to how much in benefits an executive can receive, the executives are asking for plans that will supplement the companies' retirement plans.

### Q. 9:9 Who can generally benefit under a nonqualified deferred compensation plan?

Anyone. Typically, nonqualified deferred compensation plans are designed to benefit the following:

1. Key executives;

2. A select group of management or highly compensated employees; or

3. Employees whose benefits ordinarily would be limited under Code Section 415, which limits benefits for defined contribu-

tion plans to the lesser of $30,000 (or, if greater, ¼ of the dollar limitation applicable to defined benefit plans), or 25 percent of compensation and limits benefits for defined benefit plans to the lesser of $90,000 (indexed for cost of living increases) or 100 percent of a participant's average compensation for his or her highest three consecutive years).

A nonqualified deferred compensation plan may also be designed to benefit employees who do not satisfy the requirements for participating in a qualified plan or to award employees for their services.

### Q. 9:10  Are there different types of nonqualified deferred compensation plans?

Yes, there are several types of nonqualified deferred compensation plans. The different types of plans include:

1. A "top-hat" plan (sometimes referred to as a Supplemental Executive Retirement Plan or SERP), which is, in general, an unfunded plan maintained by an employer primarily for the purpose of providing deferred compensation for a select group of management or highly compensated employees.

2. An excess benefit plan, which is a plan maintained by an employer solely for the purpose of providing benefits for certain employees in excess of the limitations on contributions and benefits imposed by Code Section 415 on plans to which that section applies, without regard to whether the plan is funded.

3. Incentive stock options, which are rights granted by the issuing corporation to an employee to purchase shares of capital stock of the corporation at a fixed price for a specified period of time. Incentive stock options meet certain statutory requirements of Code Section 422.

4. Discounted stock options, which are nonstatutory stock options that are granted at a below-market (or "discounted") exercise price.

5. A plan for governmental or tax-exempt employers under Code Section 457, which is an unfunded plan that provides for annual deferrals of the lesser of $7,500 or one-third of includable compensation (unless a $15,000 catch-up provision applies).

### Q. 9:11   How are nonqualified and qualified plans treated for tax purposes?

A nonqualified deferred compensation plan does not satisfy the requirements contained in Code Section 401(a), and as a result, does not receive the favorable tax treatment afforded plans that do satisfy those requirements. An employer contributing to a nonqualified plan will be entitled to a deduction in the year in which the amount attributable to the contribution is includable in the gross income of the participating employees, which may not be until some future date.

When a plan does satisfy the requirements under Code Section 401(a) and qualifies for the favorable tax treatment, the employer will receive an immediate tax deduction for the amount it contributes to the plan for a particular year. An employee participating in a qualified plan is not required to apply income tax on amounts contributed by the employer on his or her behalf to the plan until he or she receives these amounts at some later date. Also, the tax on the earnings on the contributions made to a qualified plan is deferred until the earnings are distributed.

*Distributions:* Plans that satisfy the requirements under Code Section 401(a) and qualify for favorable tax treatment with respect to contributions also qualify for favorable tax treatment at the time these amounts are distributed. When distributions are made from a qualified plan to a participating employee, the amounts distributed may be rolled over to another qualified plan or to an individual retirement account (IRA). These distributions may also be eligible for special tax treatment under the income averaging rules.

### Q. 9:12   Are contributions to a funded plan treated differently than contributions to an unfunded plan?

Yes. Generally contributions to an unfunded plan are not deductible by an employer and are not includable in an employee's income until some future date when the benefits are distributed or made available to the employee. Contributions to a funded plan are generally deductible by the employer and includable in an employee's income in the year the contribution is made.

### Q. 9:13 What issues need to be addressed by a company in determining the appropriateness of a deferred compensation plan?

Deferred compensation is not always the appropriate ingredient in an executive compensation program because deferred compensation is not suited for every executive. In determining whether a deferred compensation plan is appropriate for a given situation, the following questions need to be addressed:

- Is it possible that a qualified plan can be made to be more efficient than a nonqualified plan?
- Do the requirements of ERISA lessen the tax benefits or burden the plan with so many details that a qualified plan is more suitable?
- Does the executive for whose benefit the plan is being considered have a competitive current level of compensation?
- Does the executive have a reasonable expectation that the deferred income will be taxed at a lower rate in the future?
- Will the anticipated tax benefit be offset by loss of other retirement income?
- What is the level of executive confidence regarding the company's ability or future willingness to pay?
- Is the purpose of this plan to provide a better retirement plan or is it intended as golden handcuffs for a specified period of time?
- Is the executive in question a major stockholder?

### Q. 9:14 When are deferred compensation arrangements subject to FICA and FUTA taxes?

Amounts deferred under a nonqualified deferred compensation plan are subject to Federal Insurance Contributions Act (FICA) tax when the services are performed or when the executives right to such amounts are no longer subject to substantial risk of forfeiture. Most executives would prefer to have amounts that are deferred to be taxed immediately under FICA. At such time their salaries are probably already over the Social Security taxable wage base and the amounts deferred would escape FICA taxes.

If the amounts deferred are subject to a substantial risk of forfeiture, then the executive will be taxed when the risk lapses. If the deferred compensation payments vest upon retirement, then the present value of the payments expected under the deferred compensation plan will be taxable under FICA in the year of retirement assuming the Social Security wage base has not been exceeded.

The rules concerning withholding under the Federal Unemployment Tax Act (FUTA) are similar to those under FICA.

### Q. 9:15   What are the general ERISA requirements for a nonqualified deferred compensation plan?

Title 1 of ERISA contains most of the nontax requirements for nonqualified deferred compensation plans as well as employee retirement plans. Title 1 defines an employee pension plan as any plan, fund, or program established by a company that provides retirement income for employees, or results in a deferral of income by employees for periods extending to termination of employment or beyond. Because deferred compensation agreements delay payment of some of an executive's compensation until a later time (usually retirement) deferred compensation plans (unless specifically exempted) must comply with the government requirements. Fully exempted plans are governmental plans, church plans and unfunded excess benefit plans.

Unfunded deferred compensation plans maintained by a company primarily to provide deferred compensation for a select group of management or highly compensated employees must comply with the reporting and disclosure provisions of Title 1. Note, however that funded deferred compensation plans must meet all the requirements of Title 1.

ERISA requires each deferred compensation plan to provide for a claims procedure for participants and beneficiaries. The claims procedure must be described in the plan description and the summary plan description of the agreement.

### Q. 9:16   What are the general reporting and disclosure requirements for a nonqualified deferred compensation plan?

Almost all deferred compensation plans must comply with the reporting and disclosure provisions of Title 1 of ERISA. A deferred compensation plan must file a plan description with the Department of Labor (DOL) every five years and furnish a summary plan description to each covered executive or beneficiary. The summary plan description must be updated every five years if there have been plan changes or every ten years if there have been no plan changes. For unfunded or insured deferred compensation plans maintained by an company primarily to provide deferred compensation for a select group of management or highly compensated employees, the administrator can satisfy the reporting and disclosure provisions by filing, within 120 days, a general statement about the plan with the DOL.

### Q. 9:17   What are the general participation, vesting and funding requirements for a nonqualified deferred compensation plan?

Unfunded deferred compensation plans maintained by a company for the purpose of providing deferred compensation for a select group of management or highly compensated employees are excluded from participation, vesting and funding requirements of ERISA.

### Q. 9:18   What are the general fiduciary issues for a nonqualified deferred compensation plan?

Unfunded deferred compensation plans maintained by the company primarily for the purpose of providing deferred compensation for a select group of management or highly compensated employees are excluded from the fiduciary responsibilities provisions of ERISA.

### Q. 9:19　Is plan termination insurance needed for a nonqualified plan?

Unfunded deferred compensation plans maintained by the company primarily for the purpose of providing deferred compensation for a select group of management or highly compensated employees are excluded from ERISA provisions covering plan termination insurance.

## Funding Arrangements

### Q. 9:20　What is a rabbi escrow agreement?

A rabbi escrow agreement or an escrow account is another informal way of funding unfunded deferred compensation plans. Under this approach, a company guarantees deferred compensation amounts by creating an escrow fund with a financial institution as escrow agent. The company makes contributions to the account in an amount determined to be adequate to fund the benefits provided in the deferred compensation plan. As long as the assets in the account remain subject to the claims of the company's general creditors, the contributions to the account will not be includable in the executives's income. Income earned from the investment of the escrow fund can either be paid to the company or be applied toward the company's obligation. The income is taxable to the company. In all other respects, this arrangement has the same general provisions and tax consequences as the "rabbi trust" (see Q. 10:23).

### Q. 9:21　What is a "rabbi trust"?

A rabbi trust is an irrevocable trust into which assets earmarked for benefit liabilities are contributed. Trust assets typically are protected for use in meeting the benefit liabilities, but they must remain accessible to the company's general creditors in the event of bankruptcy or insolvency. The contributions and earnings are not taxable to the executives and the company does not get a deduction for its contributions. The earnings from the trusts' investments are taxable to the company.

The general creditors' access to the trust assets in the event of bankruptcy or insolvency creates an element of risk for the executives. This uncertainty is the biggest drawback of rabbi trusts. Companies, that have installed rabbi trust, tend to view the bankruptcy and insolvency risk as minimal and consider the rabbi trust as a safety net for benefits in the case of a takeover.

The primary use of rabbi trust continues to be to fund nonqualified retirement programs although they can be used as voluntary deferred arrangements. The appeal of the rabbit trust as a funding vehicle is that when properly structured, it will successfully defer income for the executive while protecting the benefit from all but general creditors. If the trust is not designed in accordance provisions accepted by IRS, however, it runs the risk that the executives may be deemed in constructive receipt of trust assets at the time the trust is funded.

IRS has issued only general principles relating to these arrangements although the concept was initially approved by IRS in a 1980 private letter ruling. Under this ruling , a congregation contributed amounts into an irrevocable trust it established for the benefit of its rabbi. IRS ruled that because the assets were subject to the general creditors of the congregation, the rabbi was not in constructive receipt of the contributions to the trust. Additional private letter rulings reinforced this concept. However, because private letter rulings are meant to apply to a specific situation, it is prudent for a company to request a private letter ruling that will ensure the validity of the arrangement.

### Q. 9:22  What is a secular trust?

Secular trusts or Section 402(b) trusts fund benefit obligations on a current basis and its assets are secured until the time of distribution to the beneficiary. Because the assets are not available to general creditors the funds in the secular trust become taxable income to the beneficiaries. When properly structured, the secular trust can provide the same after-tax benefit as a rabbi trust while costing the company less. This is due to the generally lower tax rates to which individuals are subject to and the fact that the company can gross up an executive's income to pay the tax liability attributable to the annual funding requirement.

### Q. 9:23 What is the major distinction between a secular trust and a rabbi trust?

The major difference between a secular and rabbi trust is that while creditors can claim assets held in a rabbi trust, money held in a secular trust cannot be reached by creditors.

### Q. 9:24 Can life insurance also be used by an employer to fulfill its promise to an employee?

Yes, a company may purchase insurance policies to fund its promise. These policies are referred to as corporate-owned life insurance (COLI). COLI is like-key person insurance except that a COLI contract generally covers the lives of several employees and the financial interest that the employer seeks to "insure" bears little relation to the financial loss to the corporation on the death of the covered employee.

### Q. 9:25 How is life insurance used by an employer to fulfill its promise to an employee?

A corporation will generally purchase cash value life insurance policies on individual employees and borrow against the cash value contained in the COLI policy. The cash value in a life insurance policy generates an investment income that is exempt from tax (i.e., the inside buildup) and, subject to certain restrictions, the interest paid on the loan against the cash value may be deductible. As a result, the purchase of a COLI contract makes it possible for a corporation to generate tax deductions that can be used to shelter general corporate income from tax.

The employer is the owner and beneficiary of the policies and pays the premiums. The employer will pay benefits to the employee with funds obtained from borrowing against the cash value of the policies.

## Implications of Funded and Unfunded Plans for Purposes of ERISA

### Q. 9:26   For purposes of ERISA Title I, is a nonqualified deferred compensation plan generally considered funded or unfunded?

Nonqualified deferred compensation plans generally are "unfunded" plans because they are merely promises by the employer to pay the employee compensation at some future date. However, a nonqualified deferred compensation plan may also be a "funded" plan. This occurs when a fund is created by an employer who irrevocably sets aside an amount with a third party for the benefit of an employee.

### Q. 9:27   What is the difference between a "funded" and an "unfunded" plan?

Whether or not a plan is "funded" or "unfunded" generally requires an examination of the surrounding facts and circumstances.

*Funded plans:* A plan usually will be considered "funded" if an amount is irrevocably placed with a third party for the benefit of an employee and neither the employer nor its creditors has any interest in this amount.

*Unfunded plans:* An "unfunded" plan is merely an unsecured promise by an employer to pay compensation to an employee at some future date. The employer may set aside assets in order to fulfill its promise to the employee, but the assets which are set aside must remain part of the employer's general assets and subject to the claims of the employer's creditors. The employer's promise may not be secured in any way. The participant may rely only on the credit of the employer and generally has no rights to the assets other than as a general unsecured creditor.

### Q. 9:28   For purposes of ERISA Title I, are plans affected by whether or not they are considered funded or unfunded?

Yes. If a plan is "funded," the plan will have to satisfy the requirements contained in Title I of ERISA, which pertains to participation and vesting, funding, and fiduciary requirements. If a plan is unfunded, the plan may be exempt from these requirements.

## Types of Deferred Compensation Plans

### Q. 9:29   What is a top-hat plan?

A "top-hat plan" or Supplemental Executive Retirement Plan (SERP) is a nonqualified retirement plan used to provide additional or supplemental benefits to an employer's key employees. Under the Employee Retirement Income Security Act of 1974 (ERISA), as amended ("ERISA"), a top-hat plan is generally defined as an unfunded nonqualified deferred compensation plan maintained "primarily for the purpose of providing deferred compensation for a select group of management or highly compensated employees."

### Q. 9:30   Why would an employer establish a top-hat plan?

Employers establish top-hat plans to provide additional compensation to certain employees. Prior to the TRA '86, employers established top-hat plans to allow key executives to defer compensation until retirement when, presumably, their tax rates would be substantially lower. Under the TRA '86, tax rates were reduced and the various tax brackets were essentially eliminated which, in turn, eliminated a significant benefit to deferring an executive's compensation. However, when and if Congress increases the current tax rates, the benefits achieved by deferring compensation until the recipient is in a lower tax bracket will again be significant.

In spite of the TRA '86 rate and bracket revisions, other reasons still exist for employers to establish top-hat plans. One reason is that there are significant limitations on contributions that are allowed under a qualified plan. Top-hat plans can be adopted to provide supplemental retirement income to certain highly compensated employees.

A top-hat plan, on the other hand, may be based on an executive's entire salary and provide benefits above the limits imposed by IRS.

Other reasons top-hat plans are also established include:

1. Providing a pension supplement to attract older executives where the years of service factor in a qualified retirement plan would limit such an employee's benefits;

2. Providing funds to allow an executive to retire early without losing benefits;

3. Providing an inducement for an executive to remain with the employer;

4. Providing a generous benefit package to attract desired executives; and

5. Avoiding the 10-percent tax under Code Section 72(t) on distributions made from qualified plans to an executive who is not 59½ years old.

### Q. 9:31 Does an employer inadvertently create a top-hat plan that is subject to ERISA requirements when it provides benefits to one executive under an employment contract?

Generally no. Benefits provided to one executive under an individual employment contract will ordinarily not be considered a top-hat plan. In two DOL advisory opinions, DOL ruled that contractual arrangements with individual executives were merely employment contracts and not "employee pension benefit plans" as defined by ERISA and, therefore, not subject to the requirements of ERISA.

### Q. 9:32 How does the employer pay the benefits provided by a top-hat plan?

An employer generally pays the benefits provided under a top-hat plan out of its general assets at the time the payments become due pursuant to the terms of the plan. The executive must rely solely on the employer's promise to pay these benefits and assumes the risk that these benefits may not be paid if there is an unfriendly change in the management of the employer or a change in the employer's financial situation. For example, if the employer becomes insolvent, the participating employees may not receive any benefits. In addition, where the employer is acquired in a hostile takeover, the new management team may refuse to pay the benefits promised to the employees by the former employer.

### Q. 9:33    Can employer assurances be made that future benefits will be paid without subjecting employees to current taxation?

Yes. Top-hat plans have adopted a number of informal funding arrangements to address the issue of employee assurances. They include:

1. *Corporate Owned Life Insurance:* A corporate owned life insurance policy on the life of a key executive is one method of funding the obligations provided by a top-hat plan that avoids current taxation if certain conditions are met. Under this arrangement, the tax deferred cash value build up and the tax-free receipt of death proceeds makes the use of an insurance policy an attractive funding vehicle because the policy will provide death benefits in the event the executive dies, or a cash value that the plan can borrow against in order to provide benefits to an executive on retirement. The cash value of an insurance policy used by a top-hat plan, however, will still be subject to claims of the employer's creditors and the existence of an insurance policy will not guarantee that the promised benefits will actually be paid.

2. *Rabbi Trust:* In general, the rabbi trust is an irrevocable trust that may be used to hold the assets of a top-hat plan (see Chapter 4). Typically, the rabbi trust protects an executive by providing a measure of security that the benefits promised under the top-hat plan will be paid because the assets held in the trust are not available to a corporate raider or subject to the discretion of management. In order to avoid current taxation, however, assets held in the rabbi trust remain subject to the claims of the employer's creditors in the event of the employer's insolvency or bankruptcy.

3. *Third-party guarantee:* In this arrangement, a third party guarantees payment of the benefits promised under the top-hat plan in the event the employer defaults. IRS has ruled that there are

no current tax consequences to the employee where the guarantor's promise to pay is unsecured and unfunded. This arrangement will provide adequate assurances to the employee that the benefits will be paid only where the guarantor is financially sound.

4. *Surety bonds:* Executives can purchase a surety bond to ensure that the benefits provided by a top-hat plan will be paid. IRS has ruled that the purchase of a financial surety bond by the executive to protect the executive's future deferred compensation payments may not, by itself, cause the deferred amounts to be included in the executive's income either at the time the executive purchased the bond or at the time the executive paid the premiums thereon. IRS informally indicated, however, that where surety bonds are used to protect an unfunded, unsecured promise to pay, the surety bonds may be treated as taxable property under the economic benefit doctrine.

### Q. 9:34 Are top-hat plans subject to the requirements under Title I of ERISA?

Yes. However, if a plan maintained by an employer *primarily* for the purpose of providing deferred compensation for a *select group of management or highly compensated employees* is unfunded, the plan is exempt from certain requirements of ERISA Title I.

### Q. 9:35 Is a top-hat plan a funded or unfunded plan for purposes of Title I of ERISA?

A top-hat plan is generally defined as an unfunded plan under ERISA Sections 201(2), 301(a)(3), and 401(a)(1), and generally will be unfunded if plan benefits are payable out of the employer's general assets and any participant in the plan has no greater rights in these assets than a general unsecured creditor.

Conversely, a plan will generally be considered "funded" if the assets are segregated or otherwise set aside so that such assets are identified as a source from which participants may look for the payment of their benefits.

At least one court has noted that the distinction between a funded and unfunded plan turns on whether there is a separate *res* or property that is set apart or segregated from the employer's general funds to which the employee could look in the event the contingency occurs that triggers the employer's liability of the plan.

### Q. 9:36   For purposes of Title I of ERISA, is it significant whether or not a top-hat plan is funded or unfunded?

Yes. Under Title I of ERISA, whether a top-hat plan is funded is significant. An unfunded top-hat plan is exempt from the ERISA provisions pertaining to participation and vesting, funding, and fiduciary responsibilities pursuant to the exemptions contained in ERISA Sections 201(2), 301(a)(3), and 401(a)(1). If a top-hat plan is funded, the plan will be required to comply with all of the provisions of Title I of ERISA.

### Q. 9:37   Are contributions to an unfunded top-hat plan treated differently than contributions to a funded top-hat plan?

Yes. Contributions to an unfunded top-hat plan are generally not deductible by an employer and are not includable in an employee's income until the benefits are actually distributed or made available to the employee. Employer contributions to a funded top-hat plan, however, are generally deductible by the employer and includable in the employee's income in the year the contribution is made. Note that contributions made to a funded top-hat plan that are subject to a substantial risk of forfeiture will generally not be deductible to an employer and includable in the employee's income until the benefits vest and are not subject to a substantial risk of forfeiture.

### Q. 9:38   When can an employer deduct its contribution to a top-hat plan?

An employer is generally entitled to deduct its contribution to a top-hat plan in the year in which an amount attributable to the contribution is includable in the employee's gross income.

If, on the other hand, the top-hat plan is considered to be funded, employer contributions are generally deductible in the year the contribution is made.

### Q. 9:39  When are contributions that are made to a top-hat plan includable in the employee's gross income?

It depends on whether the top-hat plan is funded or unfunded. Amounts contributed to an unfunded top-hat plan are includable in the employee's gross income at the time these amounts are paid or made available to the employee.

If the top-hat plan is considered to be funded, the amounts contributed are includable in the employee's gross income in the year the contribution is made. However, contributions to a funded top-hat plan that are subject to a substantial risk of forfeiture are generally not includable in the employee's gross income until the contributions have vested and are no longer subject to a substantial risk of forfeiture. The timing of an employee's recognition of income with respect to contributions made to a top-hat plan can be in the year of contribution if the employee comes within the constructive receipt or economic benefit doctrines.

### Q. 9:40  What is an excess benefit plan?

An excess benefit plan is a nonqualified deferred compensation plan "maintained by an employer solely for the purpose of providing benefits for certain employees in excess of the limitations on contributions and benefits imposed by Code Section 415." In simplified terms, an excess benefit plan either takes the place of a more rigid qualified plan governed by ERISA or supplements the qualified plan to provide more benefits to the participants. In addition, not only may an excess benefit plan be a separate and distinct plan itself, it may also be a separable part of a tax-qualified plan.

### Q. 9:41  How does a plan qualify as an excess benefit plan?

In order to qualify as an excess benefit plan, the sole purpose of the nonqualified plan must be limited to providing benefits to participants in excess of the limitations imposed by Code Section 415.

## Q. 9:42 Why would an employer establish an excess benefit plan?

An employer may be interested in establishing an excess benefit plan for several reasons, including:

1. Attracting certain personnel through the additional benefits provided by such plans;

2. Retaining certain employees by making the excess benefit plan a disincentive for any employee contemplating resignation;

3. Providing employees an excess benefit plan as an incentive for better service and increased productivity;

4. Creating goodwill between the employer and the participants in the excess benefit plan; and

5. Encouraging early retirement for some highly paid employees by providing them with increased benefits.

## Q. 9:43 Are there benefits to establishing an excess benefit plan?

Yes. Because an excess benefit plan is not generally governed by a strict statutory or regulatory framework (although funded excess benefit plans must meet certain ERISA requirements), an excess benefit plan offers greater flexibility because it can be drafted to meet the specific needs of the employer. An excess benefit plan is ordinarily established in concert with a qualified deferred compensation plan and the excess benefit plan provides supplemental benefits to certain employees in addition to the benefits provided under the qualified plan.

Finally, another example of the flexibility of an excess benefits plan is that it need not be based upon the number of years of service of the participant. Employees often need to be assured of receiving compensation in future years, and an excess benefit plan allows employers to provide their employees with such compensation.

## Q. 9:44 Are there limitations in establishing an excess benefit plan?

Yes. The major limitations in establishing an *unfunded* excess benefit plan relate to the tenuous position of the participant. The participant holds the status of a general, unsecured creditor with regard to the excess benefit plan benefits, and, as a result, the participant may not have any comfort that he or she will ever receive any benefits under the plan, especially if the employer is not well capitalized.

A second limitation relating to an unfunded excess benefit plan is that, unlike a qualified deferred compensation plan, the employer who establishes such an excess benefit plan generally does not receive an income tax deduction for its contributions until the contributions are actually distributed or made available to the participants, which can often be years in the future.

A third major limitation on the use of an excess benefit plan is that an excess benefit plan is expressly limited to a plan maintained *solely* for providing benefits to the plan participants in excess of the limitations imposed by Code Section 415. The term "solely" has not been clearly defined. As a result, the employer must make certain that the *sole* purpose for establishing the excess benefit plan is to provide benefits in excess of the limitations contained in Code Section 415 to protect the status of the plan as an excess benefit plan. (If the plan ceases to be considered an excess benefit plan, it may be considered a top-hat plan but it must satisfy the requirements applicable to top-hat plans.)

### Q. 9:45   Is an excess benefit plan subject to the ERISA Title I requirements?

An excess benefit plan may be subject to certain requirements under Title I of ERISA depending upon whether the plan is funded or unfunded. An excess benefit plan is defined in ERISA Section 3(36) as a plan maintained by an employer solely for the purpose of providing benefits for certain employees in excess of the limitations on contributions and benefits imposed by Code Section 415 on plans to which that section applies, without regard to whether the plan is funded. If the plan is unfunded, the plan is exempt from the requirements under Title I of ERISA. If the plan is funded, the plan is subject to certain requirements under ERISA.

### Q. 9:46  Is an excess benefit plan subject to the participation, vesting and funding requirements imposed by Title I of ERISA?

No. An excess benefit plan, whether funded or unfunded, is not subject to the participation and vesting rules of Part 2 of Title I of ERISA and the funding rules of Part 3 of Title I.

### Q. 9:47  Is an excess benefit plan subject to the reporting and disclosure requirements imposed by Title I of ERISA?

It depends on whether the plan is funded or unfunded. If the excess benefit plan is a funded plan, it will be subject to the reporting and disclosure requirements under Part 1 of Title I of ERISA. However, if the excess benefit plan is an unfunded plan, it will not be subject to such reporting and disclosure requirements.

### Q. 9:48  What is a 457 deferred plan?

Code Section 457 covers nonqualified deferral plans for not for profit organizations. This section describes the requirements that must be met in order to avoid immediate taxation to the executive for the deferred monies. These specific regulations for a nonqualified plan are often overlooked because in the profit sector nonqualified plan implies no guidelines on permissible amounts of deferral.

The maximum amount that can be deferred under this provision for any taxable year cannot exceed $7,500 or 33 percent of the executives compensation. During the last three years prior to normal retirement age the maximum amount is the lesser of $15,000 or the sum of the maximum amounts which could have been deferred but were not. The Code Section 457 maximums are reduced by any amounts deferred under qualified plans.

Compensation can be deferred for any calendar month as long as the decision is made prior to that month. All amounts of compensation deferred under this type of plan and all income from those amounts have to remain solely the property of the company and subject to the claims of creditors.

**Q. 9:49   Does Code Section 457 apply to all deferrals under governmental and tax-exempt plans?**

No. Code Section 457 does not apply to deferrals under:

1. Any Code Section 401(a) plan that includes a trust exempt from tax under Code Section 501(a);

2. A Code Section 403 annuity plan or contract;

3. That portion of any plan which consists of a property transfer described in Code Section 83; or

4. That part of a plan which consists of a trust to which Code Section 402(b) applies.


## Tax Consequences to Employers and Employees

**Q. 9:50   How are employers who establish funded excess benefit plans treated for tax purposes?**

The employer generally is entitled to deduct contributions made pursuant to the provisions of a funded plan in the year in which the contributions are made.

If, however, the participant's rights to benefits held under the plan are subject to a substantial risk of forfeiture, the employer may not be entitled to a deduction in the year the contribution is made.

In addition, the employer must maintain separate accounts for funded plans covering more than one participant in order to be entitled to a deduction.


**Q. 9:51   How are employees who benefit from excess benefit plans treated for tax purposes?**

The tax treatment to the employee depends upon whether the excess benefit plan is unfunded or funded.

**Q. 9:52   How are employees who benefit from unfunded excess benefit plans treated for tax purposes?**

Generally, amounts contributed to an unfunded excess benefit plan are includable in the employee's gross income at the time these amounts are paid or made available to the employee.

To avoid the application of the constructive receipt doctrine to excess benefit plans, which would immediately tax the employees, employers must be careful when specifying the manner of payment. Excess benefit plan provisions have often provided that the plan benefits will be paid at the same time and in the same manner as the qualified deferred compensation plan that the excess benefit plan supplements. Currently, however, this type of provision may be risky because it can cause the employee to constructively receive income if, for example, the qualified plan provides that the participant may make or change elections or may have the right to "cash-out" his or her benefit in a lump sum.

**Q. 9:53   How are employees who benefit from funded excess benefit plans treated for tax purposes?**

The employee is generally taxed concurrently with the funding of the plan, but only to the extent the participant's interest is vested. If the participant's benefits are subject to a substantial risk of forfeiture and such benefits are not transferable, the employee will not be taxed on the contributions made to fund the plan until the contributions have vested and are no longer subject to such substantial risk of forfeiture.

**Q. 9:54   When may an employer deduct its contributions to a nonqualified deferred compensation plan?**

An employer may generally deduct its contribution to a nonqualified deferred compensation plan in the year in which an amount attributable to the contribution is includable in the participating employee's gross income.

**Q. 9:55 When are contributions made to a nonqualified deferred compensation plan includable in the employee's gross income?**

Amounts contributed to a nonqualified deferred compensation plan are generally includable in the employee's gross income at the time these amounts are paid or made available to the employee.

**Q. 9:56 What is the constructive receipt doctrine for purposes of determining when income must be included in an employee's gross income?**

Generally, income, although not actually reduced to a taxpayer's possession, is constructively received by the taxpayer in the taxable year during which it is:

1. Credited to his or her account;
2. Set apart for him or her; or
3. Otherwise made available to the taxpayer.

However, income is not constructively received if the taxpayer's control over it is subject to substantial limitations or restrictions. Accordingly, if a corporation credits its employees with bonus stock, but the stock is not available to the employees until some future date, the mere crediting on the books of the corporation does not constitute receipt.

**Q. 9:57 Are contributions made pursuant to a nonqualified deferred compensation plan includable in an employee's income under the constructive receipt doctrine?**

Generally no. If the employee's control over the contributions is subject to substantial limitations, then contributions to a nonqualified deferred compensation plan should not be subject to the constructive receipt doctrine. Generally, a taxpayer includes the amount of any item of gross income in his or her gross income for the taxable year in which he or she receives it, unless, under the taxpayer's method of accounting, it is properly included in a different period. Generally, the employee, as a cash method taxpayer, includes amounts in gross income when they are actually or constructively received.

**Q. 9:58   What is the economic benefit doctrine for purposes of determining when deferred income must be included in an employee's gross income?**

The economic benefit doctrine requires that any economic or financial benefit that is conferred on an individual as compensation in a taxable year must be included in the individual's gross income in the year the benefit is conferred.

**Q. 9:59   Are contributions made pursuant to a nonqualified deferred compensation plan includable in the employee's income under the economic benefit doctrine?**

Generally no. If contributions are made or amounts set aside in accordance with a nonqualified deferred compensation plan are subject to the claims of the employer's general creditors, then such contributions or amounts should not be subject to the economic benefit doctrine. If, on the other hand, contributions to the plan are protected from the employer's creditors and the rights of the participating employees to the benefits provided under the plan are nonforfeitable, the economic benefit doctrine should apply and the contributions should be includable in the participating employee's income.

**Q. 9:60   How does Code Section 83 tax property transfers to an employee in exchange for the performance of services?**

In general, Code Section 83 provides rules for the taxation of property transferred to an employee in connection with the performance of services. This property is generally not taxable to an employee until it has been transferred to or becomes substantially vested in the employee. The application of Code Section 83 can be broken down as follows:

1. *What is a transfer of property?* A transfer of property occurs when a person acquires a beneficial ownership interest in the property.

2. *When is property substantially vested?* Property is substantially vested for purposes of Code Section 83 when it is either transferable or not subject to a substantial risk of forfeiture. A

substantial risk of forfeiture exists where rights in property that are transferred are:

- Conditioned either upon the future performance, or non-performance, of substantial services by any person, or the occurrence of a condition related to a purpose of the transfer; and

- The possibility of forfeiture is substantial if such condition is not satisfied.

3. *When are property rights transferable?* The rights of an employee in property are transferable if the employee can transfer any interest in the property to any person other than the transferor of the property, but only if the transferee's rights in the property are not subject to a substantial risk of forfeiture.

4. *What is property?* The term "property" includes, real and personal property other than money or an unfunded and unsecured promise to pay money in the future. The term also includes a beneficial interest in assets, including money, that are transferred or set aside from the claims of creditors of the transferor.

If the contributions under a nonqualified deferred compensation plan are subject to the claims of the employer's general creditors, then such contributions do not meet the definition of property. Therefore, there can be no transfer of property within the meaning of Code Section 83. If, on the other hand, contributions under a nonqualified deferred compensation plan are not available either to the employer or the employer's general creditors and the participating employees are fully vested in the contributions, then there is a transfer of property within the meaning of Code Section 83 and the employee is subject to tax on the transferred amount.

# Chapter 10

# Perquisites and Other Benefits

Executive Perquisites ("Perks") are those benefits that are above and beyond what is available to all employees. Although executive perquisites and other benefits have lost most of their tax advantages their continued use by companies is driven primarily as a status symbol for various executives and include such benefits as (1) an annual physical exam, (2) a company-provided automobile, (3) a luncheon or dining club membership, (4) a country club membership, and (5) tax and financial counseling. Additional nontraditional "benefits" such as employment contracts and golden parachute agreements are also considered executive perquisites as well. This chapter covers the common perquisites that are offered to executives.

### Q. 10:1   What is an executive perquisite?

An executive perquisite, or fringe benefit, is any enhancement of employment beyond a basic salary. This is usually considered by an executive to include expense accounts or reimbursement for travel and entertainment costs, company cars and club dues; however, to the extent these are reasonable expenses which are related to a necessary business purpose, they are technically not fringe benefits. Instead, these are expenses that may be deductible by the corporation as legitimate business expenses, and may be reimbursed to the executive without income to that executive.

## Q. 10:2   What is the tax treatment of executive perquisites?

Reasonable expenses incurred by an executive that are related to a recurring business purpose may be reimbursed without creating compensation income to the executive. (Although, see Q. 10:5 and Q. 10:6 for special rules relating to travel and entertainment expenses.) Perquisites, however, are generally deemed to be compensation and their value therefore taxable as compensation to the executive, unless they meet certain conditions which will allow them to be accorded preferred tax treatment.

Section 132 of the Code sets up certain categories of perquisites which will be accorded preferred tax treatment, that is, they will not be included in the employee's income if they are one of the following:

- Services that the employer offers to nonemployees in its usual business, where the employer incurs no additional cost in providing the service to the employee, as long as the benefit is not available only to the company's most highly compensated employees;

- Employee discounts on merchandise or services which the employer offers to nonemployees in its usual business, up to the amount of the employer's usual profit (in the case of merchandise) or 20 percent (in the case of services), as long as the benefit is not available only to the company's most highly compensated employees;

- Any property or services provided to the executive which would be deductible by the executive as a business or trade expense if the executive had paid for such property or services; or

- Property or services where the accounting for such property or services would be unreasonable or administratively impracticable. [See IRC § 132(e)(1), which provinces for this often referred to "*de minimis* exception".]

Note, however, that for a Subchapter S corporation, fringe benefits granted to an employee who owns 2 percent or more of the company's stock are generally not accorded preferred tax treatment, since those people are treated as partners.

### Q. 10:3    What is the accounting treatment of executive perquisites?

Where executive perquisites are treated as compensation to the executive, the company can deduct the cost of the benefits as a compensation expense but the company is also subject to the employer's share of any employment taxes that may be due. Where perquisites are not compensation to the executive because they are reasonable and related to a necessary business purpose, they are deductible by the company as a business expense.

### Q. 10:4    What expenses can a company generally reimburse an executive for without creating income to the executive?

Generally, a company can reimburse an executive for his out-of-pocket expenses and deduct the reimbursed amounts as a business expense as long as the expense is an ordinary and necessary cost, bearing a sufficient relationship to the company's business and reasonable in amount. [IRC §§ 162(a)(2) and 212].

### Q. 10:5    What are the special rules relating to the reimbursement of travel expenses?

The rules that determine whether travel expenses will be deductible are extremely complicated and involved. Simply stated, in order to be deductible, travel expenses must be incurred while away from home in pursuit of the company's business; if this is the case, then travel expense also includes not only transportation fares, but also the cost of meals and lodging, and related expenditures, although not entertainment expenses. [Treas Reg § 1.162-2(a)] Travel expenses must be carefully documented by the company, and thus by the executive; substantiation must be given for all expenses, and for each expense the company must be able to state the amount, the date and place incurred, and the destination and business purpose of the trip.

### Q. 10:6    What are the special rules relating to the reimbursement of entertainment expenses?

In addition to the general rule requiring that the expense be reasonable, ordinary and necessary, entertainment expenses must be either "directly related to" or "associated with" the active conduct of the company's business. An expense is "directly related" to a company's business if it involved an active discussion aimed at obtaining immediate revenue (as opposed to mere goodwill), or occurred in a clear business setting such as a hospitality room. [Treas Reg § 1.274-2(c)(2)] An expense is "associated with" a company's business if it is associated with the active conduct of the company's business and precedes or follows a substantial and bona fide business discussion. Entertainment expenses, like travel expenses, must be carefully substantiated so that the company is able to state the amount, the date and place incurred, the persons entertained (including relevant business associations), type of entertainment and its business purpose or benefit, and the nature of any business discussion or activity that took place for each expense.

### Q. 10:7    How common are expense accounts and how are they treated for tax and accounting purposes?

Expense accounts are quite common. In fact, according to a recent survey, 45 percent of the companies surveyed provided expense accounts to their executives. (See *The Officer Compensation Report—The Executive Compensation Survey for Small and Medium Sized Businesses, Twelfth Edition.*) The amount of the expense account will be taxable income to the executive except to the extent the executive submits receipts to the company. Whether a company will agree to reimburse an executive for all or a portion of his reasonable, ordinary, necessary and vouchered expenses, or for some nondeductible entertainment expenses as well, almost all companies have some form of expense account system.

### Q. 10:8    How common are club membership payments and how are they treated for tax and accounting purposes?

Club membership payments are also one of the most common executive perquisites. In fact, according to a recent survey, 32 percent of the companies surveyed provided club memberships to their executives. (See *The Officer Compensation Report—The Executive Compensation Survey for Small and Medium Sized Businesses, Twelfth Edition.*) Such payments are a form of entertainment expense and, in order to be deductible, the executive must use the club primarily for business. Club dues and membership fees paid to professional or business clubs are deductible if the expense is ordinary and necessary; club dues and membership fees paid to a social or athletic club are considered to be a form of entertainment expense and must meet those rules in order to be deductible by the corporation and not compensation to the executive.

### Q. 10:9   How common are company car programs and how are they treated for tax and accounting purposes?

Company car programs are also one of the most common executive perquisites. In fact, according to a recent survey, 41 percent of the companies surveyed provided company cars to their executives. (See *The Officer Compensation Report—The Executive Compensation Survey for Small and Medium Sized Businesses, Twelfth Edition.*) Transportation expenses are deductible by the company if they are directly attributable to its business; however, commuting costs are a nondeductible personal expense of the executive. A car allowance provided by the company will constitute income to the executive to the extent the allowance exceeds his actual costs in using the car for company business.

### Q. 10:10   What are some other benefits that a company may want to provide to its executives despite the tax consequences?

A company can choose to provide such additional benefits as payment for an executive's relocation expenses as well as provide them with an incentive hiring bonus, employment agreements, life insurance, enhanced medical benefits plans, interest-free or low-interest loans, severance compensation, and golden parachute agreements, to name a few.

### Q. 10:11   What is a hiring bonus and why would a company pay a hiring bonus?

A hiring bonus is a one-time payment used by companies to entice an executive into accepting employment by compensating him or her for concerns that are not related to specific job qualifications or experience. Such concerns include compensating executives for relocating into less desirable geographic locations, accepting a lower initial base salary, or simply agreeing to change positions.

### Q. 10:12   Is company-provided life insurance taxable to the executive?

The cost of company provided life insurance is taxable income to the executive unless the insurance is provided under a group-term policy. Under a group-term policy, the benefit is tax-free only up to $50,000 of coverage. The cost of additional insurance is taxable income to the executive and the amount of this taxable income is not the amount the company actually pays for the coverage but which is the amount based on an IRS table of coverage or "uniform premiums."

### Q. 10:13   What is split-dollar life insurance?

Split-dollar life insurance is a form of executive compensation that has been popular for many years. It is an arrangement that provides for the company and the executive to "split" the cost of the executive's life insurance. The advantage of the split-dollar approach is that it allows the company to provide the executive with life insurance at a minimal cost to the executive. While there are several variations on the split-dollar approach, the typical approach involves a situation where the company receives all of the rights under the policy except the right to designate the beneficiary. The company and the executive agree to split the premium cost although the actual split depends on both the insurance product and the level of desired spending. Typically, the company pays the great majority or all of the premium and at the time of the executive's death, the company receives an amount equal to the cash surrender value of the policy and the balance of the proceeds goes to the beneficiary that was designated by the executive.

**Q. 10:14   Can a split-dollar arrangement be used in situations other than between employers and employees?**

Yes. While a split-dollar arrangement usually involves an employer and an employee, such an arrangement may also be structured between individuals, a shareholder and a corporation, or an individual and any entity having an insurable interest in the individual.

**Q. 10:15   Can a company take out additional insurance on an executive with itself as the beneficiary?**

Yes. This is often called key-man insurance. It is not an executive perquisite, however, because only the company benefits from the insurance, not the executive.

**Q. 10:16   In what ways does a company benefit from key-man insurance?**

Life insurance held by a company on a key executive can benefit the company in the following ways:

- The proceeds of the insurance will provide the firm with an amount to compensate for the loss suffered by the executive's death;
- The payment of the annual premiums is an orderly accumulation of a fund with an increasing cash surrender value that provides an accumulation of funds that can be used for emergencies;
- The administrative expense of a private investment fund is avoided;
- The safety of the fund is insured through the insurance company; and
- The accumulation fund may strengthen the credit of the company by providing collateral for loans.

**Q. 10:17   What is the financial planning perquisite?**

This perquisite requires the company to pay outside consultants to provide personal financial planning services for executives. These services typically cover income tax planning and preparation, investment advice, guidance on obtaining the full advantage of compensation and executive benefits, retirement counseling, and estate planning.

In most cases, IRS treats the fee paid by the company as taxable income to the executive. However, to the extent that the fee is paid for tax counsel or in connection with the preparation of tax returns, or for investment counsel in connection with investments held for income production, it is also probably deductible by the executive. Where this is not the case, in many cases companies "gross-up" the executive's compensation to cover any additional tax liability.

### Q. 10:18   How common is it to offer low-interest or interest free loans to executives?

Prior to the Tax Reform Act of 1984 (TRA '84), interest free loans were a common executive perquisite. Currently, however, loans of over $10,000 are subject to regulations. With certain exceptions, if a company grants a loan in excess of $10,000 to an executive, the executive must report as taxable income the difference between the established federal rate and the actual interest charged by the company on the loan.

From a tax point of view, the entire compensation portion of a below-market loan is taxable and deductible in the year in which the loan is made. However, for a below-market demand loan where the low interest rate is conditioned on future performance by the employee, the compensation portion is taxed and deducted over the life of the loan, with each year based on the amount of compensation deemed earned during each year.

### Q. 10:19   What are the advantages of giving an executive an employment agreement?

The primary advantage to a company of giving an executive an employment agreement is the resulting opportunity to include a restrictive covenant, that is, an agreement by the executive not to compete with his employer, which will come into effect upon the termination of the agreement.

### Q. 10:20   Are there disadvantages of giving an executive an employment agreement?

The primary disadvantage from the company's perspective of entering into an employment agreement with an executive is the resulting obligation to employ that executive in the agreed position during the full term of the agreement. Of course, this is the primary advantage from the executive's perspective, as it guarantees his employment during that term.

### Q. 10:21   How enforceable is a contractual agreement as to a fixed term of employment?

A contractual agreement as to a fixed term of employment is not specifically enforceable against the executive. If the executive quits, the company cannot go to court to enforce the agreement because a court will not require an employee to continue to provide services against his will (although the corporation would be entitled to cease making payments under the agreement). However, the fixed term of employment is enforceable against the employer company in the sense that the company must continue to fulfill its payment obligations as set forth in the agreement throughout the term of the agreement. Generally, the only way a company can terminate an employment agreement before its expiration is if the executive has engaged in the kind of conduct that allows the corporation to terminate for "cause." Often the agreement itself will define the meaning of "cause" and the most typical definitions include a material breach by the executive of the provisions of the agreement. Where "cause" is not defined, the company must rely on its state's common law rules as to what conduct constitutes "cause."

### Q. 10:22   How enforceable is a noncompetition agreement?

A noncompetition agreement must be reasonable in order to be enforced and reasonableness is measured by the extent of the restriction and the length of time it covers. Each of these variables is measured differently in each state. As a whole, though, a restriction that prohibits the executive from engaging in the employer's business is generally disfavored by the courts. However, a restriction against soliciting company clients or employees is more likely to be enforced.

## Q. 10:23   Is severance compensation an employee perquisite?

Severance compensation is an executive perquisite in much the same way as is an employment agreement because it gives the executive a guarantee of certain payments in the event his or her employment is terminated by the company. Severance compensation which is paid to a top-level executive because of termination resulting from a change in control will be governed by the rules affecting golden parachutes even if the severance agreement makes no reference to the change in control.

## Q. 10:24   What is a golden parachute?

A golden parachute is an agreement that provides a generous severance package to top executives in the event of a change in control of the company, such as resulting from a takeover or merger. A golden parachute can be either "single trigger" or "double trigger." A single trigger agreement allows the executive to receive the stated severance benefits even if he or she voluntarily leaves following a change in control; the change in control is therefore the only "trigger" necessary to assure the executive of benefits if he or she wants them. A double trigger agreement requires that the executive's employment be terminated by the new management following the change in control, either directly or through an adverse change in working conditions which amount to a constructive termination.

## Q. 10:25   What constitutes a "change in control"?

The severance agreement will generally define the term "change in control." Its primary elements are usually the acquisition of a stated percentage of voting stock, generally between 20 percent and 50 percent, and a change in a majority of the Board of Directors.

## Q. 10:26   Why do companies provide golden parachutes?

Many companies feel that parachute programs are appropriate because they encourage key personnel who might otherwise resign for fear of losing their positions in the event of a takeover to remain with the company. These companies also argue that it is in the best interest of the company and its shareholders, employees and customers that the company not be taken over and that golden parachute programs reduce the likelihood that such a takeover will occur. In either event, companies continue to treat payments under golden parachute contracts as an ordinary and necessary trade or business expense.

### Q. 10:27   Are there criticisms of golden parachute programs?

Yes. Many individuals, including governmental officials, feel that in many instances golden parachute contracts do little but assist an entrenched management team to remain in control and/or provide corporate funds to subsidize officers and other highly paid executives. In fact, the government has concluded that a tax penalty should be exacted in certain situations in order to prevent the tax law from being used as a subsidy for entrenched management or other highly compensated executives (see Q. 10:26).

### Q. 10:28   What penalties has the government imposed on golden parachutes?

A payment to an officer, director or highly compensated individual will be deemed to be a parachute payment if it is contingent upon a change in control of the corporation and the total present value of all such contingent compensation exceeds 299 percent of the "base amount," that is, the individual's average annual compensation during the five tax years immediately prior to the change in control. For these purposes, an executive is a highly compensated individual if he is among the highest paid 1 percent of the employees or, if less, one of the highest paid 250 employees of the company.

Once it has been established that a parachute payment exists, the corporation will not be entitled to deduct that part of the payment which constitutes an "excess parachute payment" and the individual receiving the payment will be subject to a 20 percent excise tax on the excess.

The parachute provisions do not apply to "small business corporations," which are corporations that have elected subchapter S status or who are eligible to do so, nor to closely held corporations whose stock is not readily tradeable and whose stockholders have approved the severance agreements by more than a 75 percent vote with "adequate disclosure" of all material facts. However, for nonpublic corporations, the reason for adopting parachute agreements is not as compelling because management generally controls more than a majority of the stock and it is unlikely that the company will find itself in a hostile takeover situation.

### Q. 10:29  What is an "excess parachute payment?"

An excess parachute payment is any payment that exceeds the base amount. The distinction between a parachute payment and an excess parachute payment is an important one because while a parachute payment exists if payments aggregate to more than three times the base amount, once a parachute payment is found to exist, all payments above the base amount are deemed to be excess.

### Q. 10:30  Is there any way to avoid the negative impact of the excess parachute payment?

Yes. Many companies install a "fail-safe" provision in their severance compensation agreements, in the form of a paragraph that states that any amounts that may be paid to an executive that would otherwise be parachute payments should be treated as a loan by the company, repayable by the executive.

### Q. 10:31  What is a tin parachute?

Some companies have adopted parachute programs that provide payments to a large segment of, or even all employees, in the event of a change in control. These programs are designed to compensate individuals who are not officers or directors or highly compensated individuals and, as a result, are not subject to the golden parachute restrictions. The benefits provided are usually far less than under the golden parachutes, yet because they are provided to a far larger number of employees, the aggregate amount is more substantial and more likely to scare off a potential acquiror.

# Chapter 11

# Board of Directors' Compensation

Public attention has intensified its focus on the roles, responsibilities and performance of the Board of Directors. Director positions are becoming more difficult to fill given the increased liability and time demands associated with corporate governance. This in turn has increased the importance of director compensation. Both the amounts and forms of compensation have changed significantly over the past several years. The most common forms of director compensation, annual retainers and per meeting fees, are increasing in the amount paid. The prevalence of stock-based plans and retirement plans for directors is also increasing. This chapter covers the current trends and issues in board compensation.

**Q. 11:1  How does a company choose the members of its Board of Directors?**

Directors of a company are elected by the stockholders of that company. In private companies, the major stockholders usually function as executive officers and directors. In public companies, stock ownership plays a much smaller factor in the election of officers and directors; however, the Board of Directors remains primarily filled by top management, supplemented by at least two "outside" directors.

### Q. 11:2    Why would a company choose to have outside directors?

As discussed earlier, an employee benefit plan must be administered by disinterested directors in order to take advantage of the Rule 16b-3 exemption, which provides that grants of stock options and other securities under a plan to insiders will not be deemed to be purchases of those securities for purposes of determining Section 16(b) liability. In order to be disinterested, a director cannot be or have been granted or awarded stock or options under any discretionary company plan while he or she acts as a director or one year prior to becoming a director. Companies do not want to exclude their top management from participating in benefit plans in order to meet the "disinterested" standard because they are the very people that the company most desires to motivate and retain through the use of the mechanism of executive compensation. Therefore, a company will ask people who do not work for the company—well-qualified "outsiders"—to sit on its Board of Directors and pay them a special retainer and per-meeting fees.

Even for privately-held companies for whom the Section 16 exemption is not relevant, disinterested directors are useful as a mechanism to insulate the company against shareholder derivative challenges to the amounts or types of executive compensation paid because courts apply the business judgement rule to the compensation decisions made by disinterested directors. Specifically, courts will assume that the disinterested directors used their best business judgement in deciding on the compensation paid.

### Q. 11:3    What are the typical compensation elements for directors?

Most companies compensate their directors with some combination of annual retainers for their services and additional fees for their attendance at the actual meetings of the Board. Many companies have also established certain special stock plans for their directors and others give directors retirement benefits after a minimum period of service. Very few provide other benefits to their directors merely for serving as directors.

## Q. 11:4  Are "inside" directors compensated specifically for their activities as directors?

Directors who are also executive officers of a corporation are usually not given additional compensation such as annual retainers or meeting fees for acting as directors, although many companies adjust the base salaries of their executives who also serve on the Board.

## Q. 11:5  How much do "outside" directors receive for their services?

The size of retainer and meeting fees paid to an outside director varies greatly from company to company. Unfortunately, it is impossible to statistically isolate the factors that determine the level of compensation accorded to directors, although the size of the company in question is one indicator. The average retainer fee is between $16,000 and $20,000 while the typical meeting fees range from $700 to $1,000 per meeting. Statistically, this means that the average director receives less than 5 percent of the compensation paid to a chief executive officer of a Fortune 500 company. In addition, some companies also provide additional retainer and/or meeting fees for service on a committee of the Board. A typical committee retainer ranges between $2,000 and $5,000 while typical meeting fees run between $500 and $700 per meeting.

Note that the director may elect to defer receipt of these fees until a future date as agreed with company. Similarly, the company may wish to pay the outside director his or her retainer in the form of discounted stock options.

## Q. 11:6  How is director income taxed?

Directors are taxed on the amounts paid to them by the company as on all other income. However, outside directors are not considered employees of the company, and therefore the company need not withhold for taxes and Social Security payments from their fees. Instead, a director's income is considered self-employment income. This is the case whether he or she receives a retainer or fees for attending meetings or serving on committees.

### Q. 11:7   What methods are used in deferring compensation for directors?

There are two principal methods a company will use in deferring compensation of its board members. The most common method is simply to defer payment of the retainer and annual fees—as well as the taxes on such compensation—until a future date, which is typically retirement from the board or some other event. Another method is to allow a director to invest his deferred compensation in units of phantom stock with the dividends credited on the purchased units being reinvested in additional units.

### Q. 11:8   What types of performance based plans do directors participate in?

Under the new Section 16 rules, which are much more liberal than the old rules, a director's disinterested status will not be affected by his or her (1) merely being eligible to participate in a plan, (2) participation in a nondiscretionary plan, (3) participation in a participant-directed exempt plan, or (4) election to receive the annual retainer fee in securities.

A growing number of companies are offering the opportunity to participate in capital accumulation plans to their directors. The company's rationale for doing this is similar to its motives for adopting plans for its officers and employees, which is to provide incentives to people who are performing services for the company by giving them the chance to participate in the growth that their performance and decisions may cause.

Incentive stock options (ISOs) may only be granted by a corporation to its employees so that options granted to outside directors must be nonstatutory. Nonstatutory options granted to outside directors are subject to the same tax rules as options granted to regular employees.

### Q. 11:9   How are below market options used in compensating directors?

As stated earlier, many companies offer directors the option to receive their annual retainer in the form of discounted stock options.

In such a case, the fee is equal to the amount of the "spread" involved. For example, instead of paying a $10,000 fee to a director, a company would grant that director options to purchase 500 shares of stock with a market value of $12,500 ($25 per share) at a purchase price of $5 per share, or a total purchase price of $2,500 ($5 per share).

There are several significant benefits to using discounted stock options. From the director's point of view, he or she is taxed either way on the compensation element, or the amount of the spread, yet that director has effectively invested in stock using pre-tax dollars. Using the example above, assume that the director involved is in the 31 percent federal income tax bracket and a 10 percent state income tax bracket. Had that director received the $10,000 retainer in cash only $5,900 would have been left after taxes. Taking that $5,900 plus the additional $2,500 paid to exercise the options the director would have been able to purchase a total of only $8,400 in company stock. On the other hand, by choosing to receive discounted stock options the director received $12,500 in stock for which a total of $6,600 (the $2,500 exercise price plus taxes of $4,100) was paid. As for the company, it has not only saved the cash it would have had to pay the director but it will also receive cash when the director exercises the option. In addition, the company has succeeded in giving the director a personal interest in the company that is more closely aligned with the interests of the company's stockholders.

### Q. 11:10  How do the Section 16 rules apply to directors' below market options?

The decision to receive the annual fee or retainer in the form of discounted options is considered a purchase for purposes of Section 16 and is matchable against any sale by that director of company securities within the six months before or after that purchase.

### Q. 11:11  Do companies provide "regular" stock plans for directors?

Yes. Many companies allow their directors to participate in restricted stock plans and tie the vesting of the stock to years of service on the board. Remember, though, that a director is not disinterested as to any plan in which he or she participates.

### Q. 11:12    Can tandem SARs/stock options be granted to directors?

Yes. Tandem SARs/stock options may be granted to directors and the SARs will be taxed in the same manner as if they were granted to company executives.

### Q. 11:13    What other benefits are typically provided to directors?

Most publicly-traded companies will provide its outside directors with liability insurance and expense reimbursement, while others may also provide additional benefits such as medical insurance, life insurance and/or retirement plans. The rationale for providing limited benefits, simply stated, is that the outside directors are not employees of the company but were asked to be directors as a result of their corporate expertise in their primary jobs, which provide them with the coverage they require.

### Q. 11:14    Do companies provide retirement benefits for their directors?

Many companies choose to provide directors with a special retirement plan. Companies usually make the benefit payable at age 65 or the normal retirement date, which is often later than age 65.

A typical retirement plan for an outside director would include provisions such as:

- A minimum service requirement for eligibility;
- Increasing benefit levels based on the number of years, over the minimum number, served as a director;
- A maximum benefit level equal to a specified percentage, often approaching 100 percent, of the retainer; and
- Forfeiture of rights if the director competes with or otherwise harms the company.

### Q. 11:15    Can Keogh plans be utilized by outside board members?

Outside directors are considered to be self-employed, independent contractors and therefore are eligible to create a tax qualified retirement plan (i.e., Keogh plan). They can contribute a portion of their fees to the plan, generally up to 13.04% of the director's net self-employment income. Larger deductions are available in some cases. Investment income on the amount contributed builds up tax deferred with the director paying tax only as he/she receives payment.

### Q. 11:16   Can Keogh plans be utilized by insider board members?

Even where a company chooses to pay its inside directors special fees for serving as directors, IRS regulations prevent an insider board member (who is not considered a self-employed individual) from participating in a Keogh plan.

# Glossary

**Actuarial Assumptions:** Assumptions about or estimates of future experience in those areas that will affect benefit levels and costs, such as interest, pay increases, mortality, turnover, disability, and age at retirement.

**Airline Club Memberships:** Company paid memberships to hospitality clubs sponsored by airlines in airports.

**Alternative Minimum Tax:** The alternative minimum tax (AMT) is a method of calculating an executive's tax liability that ensures that all executives at high income levels bear at least a minimum level of federal tax burden.

**Annual Incentives:** Annual incentives or short-term incentives are incentives paid to executives for their performance over periods up to one year.

**Annual Physical Exam:** Company pays for these exams, usually as part of an executive wellness program designed to identify potential health problems. Most company medical insurance plans do not cover non-illness-related physical exams.

**Annuity:** One of several possible vehicles for funding a SERP. An annuity consists of a series of periodic payments, that may be of equal value or adjusted according to an index, such as the cost-of-living index. Payments typically continue for the lifetime of the recipient.

**Appreciation Plans:** Capital appreciation plans grant the executive the right to receive the value of the appreciation of price of the employer's stock.

**Base Salary:** Base salary is the amount of fixed cash compensation that is paid to an executive on a periodic basis.

**Bonus in Lieu of Company Car:** The executive receives a bonus which can be used for any purchase at his or her discretion in lieu of a company car or car allowance. This type of bonus is often applied when a company is phasing out a car program and is "buying" the car program participants out of the plan.

**Bridge Loan:** A loan to an executive that represents the amount of equity the executive has in his or her present residence. A bridge loan is made to an executive prior to the sale of the individual's residence to facilitate the purchase of a new home. Bridge loans are generally made for a limited period of time and are payable upon the sale of the primary residence.

**Business Class Flight Privileges:** Executive travels on company business in the business class section of an airplane.

**Capital Accumulation Plan (nonqualified):** A pension plan that does not meet the requirements of the Internal Revenue Code (generally, those of Section 401(k)). Employers are not permitted to deduct their contributions for benefits until the benefits are actually provided to the plan participant.

**Capital Accumulation Plan (qualified):** A pension plan that meets the requirements of the Internal Revenue Code (generally, those of Section 401(a)). Qualified plans are eligible for special tax considerations. Employers are permitted to deduct their contributions to the plan even though the benefits provided are deferred to a later date.

**Capital Gains Rate:** The capital gains tax rate was a preferential tax rate that was intended to encourage risk-taking by investors. As a result, certain profits from specified categories of property were taxed at a lower rate than other forms of income if the property was held by the investor for at least six months. The capital gains rate was effectively repealed in 1987 but remains important because capital gains can still be offset by capital losses up to $3,000.

**Car Allowance:** Executive is given an allowance that can be used either to purchase or lease a car. Many companies that once maintained car programs are moving toward giving car allowances to their executives. This enables the company to sponsor its executives with a vehicle and removes the cost and administrative work associated with maintaining company owned vehicles.

**Cash-or-Deferred Plan:** A qualified profit sharing or stock bonus plan that gives a participant an option to take cash or to have the employer contribute the money to a qualified profit sharing plan as an employer contribution to the plan (i.e. an elective deferral).

**Cellular Telephone:** Company provides telephone in car and pays for the monthly service and business related calls. Personal calls made by the executive generally are not paid for by the company.

**Cliff Vesting:** All benefits accrue to a recipient at once after a predetermined period of time. Recipients accrue no benefits until the predetermined period of time has passed. If they leave the company or are terminated prior to the vesting date, no partial benefits are received.

**Closely-Held Corporation:** A company in which management and ownership are substantially the same, that is, the company's stock is "held closely" by a few individuals.

**Co-Insurance Waiver:** Company pays the cost of co-insurance plans, which has the effect of providing the executive with individual medical coverage at significantly reduced personal cost.

**Company Car:** Automobile provided to company executive for use in company related activities. Personal use of company-provided vehicles is treated as additional tax related income and must be accounted for at the end of the tax year.

**Company Credit Card:** Credit card provided to the executive to pay for company related business and entertainment expenses. Company generally pays all fees and associated expenses related to maintenance of the credit card. Use of a company credit card enables the holder to spend money on company business without having to tie up the individual's own funds or credit.

**Company Designated Physician/Clinic:** Executive annual physicals are conducted by a doctor and/or clinic that has been selected by the company. These physical exams are not related to an examination by a physician in connection with an illness; they are preventive in nature and are not normally covered by most medical insurance plans.

**Constructive Receipt:** Constructive receipt is deemed to occur when the benefit recipient is eligible to receive or to draw upon the deferred compensation. Under IRS regulations, once an individual has taken constructive receipt of the funds, the compensation becomes taxable. The taxability of these funds is not affected by the recipient's decision not to take or draw upon the deferred funds.

**Contributory Plan:** A pension plan under which employee contributions are required as a condition of participation.

**Country Club Membership:** Company pays for membership to a club that has recreational and/or meeting facilities at which company business can be conducted. Depending upon the level of the executive, the company may pay for membership to more than one club.

**Deductible Waiver:** The company pays all deductibles specified under the medical plan, effectively providing the executive with medical coverage at significantly reduced personal cost.

**Defined Benefit Pension Plan:** Pension plan designed to provide participants with a definite benefit at retirement (e.g., a monthly benefit of 20 percent of compensation upon reaching age 65). Contributions to the plan are made in accordance with actuarial calculations based on the expected level of benefits.

**Defined Contribution Pension Plan:** Pension plan that provides an individual account for each participant. The size of the pension is based upon the amount of funds accumulated in the account from company contributions and investment performance. In contrast to the provisions of a defined benefit plan, the plan participants are not guaranteed a definite benefit upon retirement.

**Dependent Coverage Waiver:** Company pays the deductible for dependents of the executive who are covered by the company medical plan, effectively providing the executive with medical coverage for the entire family that is covered, to a very significant degree, by the employer.

**Discretionary Expense Account:** Expense account provided to an executive that is not earmarked for any specific expense. Generally executives eligible for these expense accounts have broad discretion in how and where they entertain, and are allowed to exceed the normal travel and entertainment spending levels that apply to the general employee population.

**Discrimination:** Discrimination occurs when a plan favors a certain class of employees through its provisions or operations. Generally this group includes officers, executives, shareholders, or highly compensated employees.

**Disqualification:** Loss of qualified (tax-favored) status by a plan. This generally occurs when a plan is not conducted in compliance with the tax codes or discriminates against the general employee population.

**Dollar Limit for Annual Physical Examination:** The amount of money that an executive will be reimbursed for an annual physical examination. Physical examinations are not normally covered by most medical insurance plans. This reimbursable represents a special benefit to the recipient.

**Earmarking:** Executives covered by defined contribution pension plans may direct the investment of the amounts in their accounts. In a defined contribution pension plan, there is no guaranteed benefit for the executive: The amount of the pension benefit is directly related to the sum of (1) the amount of contributions made to the plan and (2) the return from the investments in which the contributions have been invested.

**Education Loan:** Loan provided to an executive to cover expenses for additional education. Education programs eligible for these loans include professional certification, continuing education courses, and degree and/or certificate programs.

**Education Tuition Assistance:** Continuing education assistance program provided to enable an individual to get additional training in a field or a degree. In order to receive company reimbursement for courses taken, there is usually a minimum grade level that must be attained by the employee. Assistance may also include payment for books and other course related expenses and fees. Tuition assistance is a taxable benefit to the executive and is considered to be additional income from a personal tax perspective.

**Effective Tax Rate:** The effective rate is the rate the executive pays on all of his or her taxable income.

**Employment Contract:** Executive employment contracts specify certain rights and obligations for both the executive and the employer. These contracts usually define the compensation package and performance expectations, and are generally in effect for a set period of time; however, many contracts have automatic renewal clauses.

**ERISA:** The Employee Retirement Income Security Act of 1974 (ERISA) is the law designed to protect the rights of beneficiaries of employee benefit plans. The law imposes various qualification standards and fiduciary responsibilities on welfare benefit and retirement plans, and identifies enforcement procedures.

**Estate Planning:** Company provides professional financial and legal expertise to assist with financial arrangement and disposition of the individual's estate. This assistance may be provided by either financial planners and attorneys who have been retained by the company or by independent financial planners and attorneys who have been chosen by the executive.

**Fiduciary:** Any person who exercises discretionary authority or control over the management of plan assets or who gives investment advice to the plan for a fee or other consideration.

**Forfeitures:** Benefits that a plan participant loses if the participant terminates employment before becoming eligible for full retirement benefits under the plan.

**401(k) Company Contribution:** Contribution made by company to individual plan participant account. These contributions are usually vested to the plan participant over a period of time, and are sometimes made to encourage lower-salaried employees to become plan participants to help offset the impact of higher paid plan participants. If the company fails discrimination tests in which the contributions of the top one third of the salaried workforce must be balanced by the contributions of the lower two thirds, high-salaried participants may be restricted from making contributions.

**401(k) Savings Plan:** A savings plan that meets the requirements of IRC Section 401(k). Covered employees can elect to defer income by making pre-tax contributions to a profit-sharing or stock bonus plan. Contributions to these savings plans are subject to special rules and may be limited if the plan fails a discrimination test based on the contributions of non-highly paid employees that comprise the general employee population.

**Funding:** Accumulating money or other assets that can be used to pay for plan benefits, for example, by creating a welfare benefit trust or other welfare benefit fund.

**Gasoline Credit Card:** Credit cards used to purchase gasoline and/or service for a company car or for company related travel in a personal car.

**General Investment Advice:** Executive is provided with investment advice and assistance paid for by the company. Counseling normally relates to maximizing the individual's return on investment vehicles that are provided by the company and individual investments paid for by the executive. This service may be rendered by an investment counselor retained by the company or one chosen by the executive.

**Group Health Plan:** Group health plans provide medical care to participants and beneficiaries, either directly or indirectly (e.g. insurance). Under the IRC, a plan maintained by an employer to provide medical care, directly or indirectly, to employees, ex-employees, and their families. Such plans are subject to ERISA.

**Group Term Life Insurance:** A plan qualifying under IRC Section 79 that provides employees with employer-paid life insurance coverage at little or no tax cost. Employees have taxable income only to the extent that (1) the cost of insurance providing a group term general death benefit exceeds the cost of providing $50,000 of coverage or (2) the plan contains nonqualifying features. Special rules may apply to highly compensated or key employees.

**Health Club Membership:** Company paid membership to a health club. Many companies actively encourage their executives to maintain a regular fitness program under the assumption that physical fitness programs contribute to good health and will lead to lower medical expenses.

**Highly Compensated Employee:** An employee who is paid over $75,000 a year (or $50,000 if that amount places the employee in the top 20 percent of earnings paid by the employer); or a 5 percent owner or an officer paid more than 50 percent of the defined-benefit limit set by IRC Section 415(b)(1)(A). IRC Section 89, and various other provisions, bar benefit plan discrimination in favor of highly compensated employees.

**Home Entertainment:** Reimbursement of expenses incurred by an individual for company related entertainment at the person's residence or other private property. This is normally paid in one of two ways: (1) The individual is reimbursed for specific expenses as they occur or (2) An allowance is paid on a regular basis to cover the costs of recurring business related entertainment expenses.

**Home Use of Company Long Distance Service:** Company arranges for the individual to receive the corporate volume discount at the person's private residence; the individual also may be permitted to make long distance calls from the residence through the company telephone system.

**Insurance Advice:** Assistance provided to the executive on establishing a personal insurance program. Such counseling usually integrates the company plans with individual insurance plans to establish a comprehensive insurance program tailored to the individual needs of the executive.

**Key Employee:** A key employee may be defined in any of the following ways: an officer who earns more than 150 percent of the defined-benefit limit; a 5 percent direct or indirect owner of the employer; a 1 percent direct or indirect owner of the employer receiving compensation greater than $150,000 from the employer; a ½ percent owner of the employer (if this is one of the ten largest holdings) who earns more than the defined-contribution limit under IRC Section 415; or a person who was a key employee at retirement or separation from service.

**Loan Repayment at Termination:** Upon termination from company for any reason, the executive is required to repay all outstanding loans made to the employee by the company. This repayment may be due immediately upon termination, or a negotiated settlement may be arranged that converts all outstanding loans into normal installment loans. Loan interest rates and terms generally conform to prevailing market rates, terms, and conditions.

**Lunch Club Membership:** Company pays membership to a lunch club to ensure that executives have an appropriate place to entertain business clients and contacts and can obtain services not readily available in a public restaurant.

**Marginal Tax Rate:** The marginal tax rate is the rate the executive pays on the last dollar that is earned.

**Mortgage:** Mortgage provided to an employee by the employer at favorable rates and terms. Normally used for the purchase of a primary residence. Mortgage is either directly extended by the employer or arranged through a bank with the employer paying most or all of the fees related to the purchase of the mortgage.

**Nondiscrimination Rules:** Rules that may deny the employer and the employee certain tax benefits if the plan is found to discriminate in favor of highly compensated or key employees.

**Nonqualified Capital Accumulation Plans:** A pension plan that does not meet the requirements of the IRC (generally Section 401(a)), under which employers may not deduct contributions for benefits until they are provided to the plan participant. Employers use various nonqualified capital accumulation plans to supply increased or special benefits to specific employees that would be considered discriminatory under a qualified plan.

**Ordinary Income:** Ordinary income is reportable income that does not qualify as capital gains.

**Operating Funds:** Funds derived from company profits.

**Operating Funds as Funding Vehicle for SERP:** Company pays its SERP related obligations out of the annual operating budget. Companies use this form of funding when they believe that their cash flow will be sufficient to meet any retirement program related expenses out of cash flow as they occur rather than use other funding vehicles (life insurance, rabbi trusts, secular trusts, and annuities).

**Organizational Level:** The position occupied by a particular job within the organizational structure of the company. Organizational level is normally described in terms of a job's position in the company relative to the CEO. Eligibility to receive perquisites is normally tied to the organizational level of an individual's job.

**Outplacement:** Company provides a terminated executive with assistance in locating new employment. Services provided to the terminated executive typically include career counseling, assessment of strengths and weaknesses, resume preparation, interview coaching, and use of the outplacement firm's office facilities.

**Paid Attendance at Professional Meetings:** Company pays for the executive to attend meetings and conventions held by professional associations. Expenses covered include convention fees and all costs related to travel and entertainment.

**Pay for Spouse Accompanying Executive:** All travel expenses related to a spouse traveling on company business are paid by the company.

**Perquisite:** Benefits awarded to employees on a very selective basis. Eligibility to receive perquisites is often linked to specific jobs at the executive level. Traditionally, perquisites have not been linked to individual or corporate performance. Once awarded, a perquisite is very seldom taken away from an individual executive.

**Personal Computer at Home:** Executive is provided with a personal computer that can be used at home for company business.

**Personal Residence Sale or Purchase:** Company assists an executive in buying or selling a personal residence to facilitate relocating to take a job with the company. Normally this benefit is applicable only to an executive's primary residence; summer and vacation homes are not included.

**Post Retirement AD&D Insurance:** Accidental death and disability insurance coverage provided by employer to executive after retirement.

**Post Retirement Annual Physical:** Company pays for an annual physical for retired executives.

**Post Retirement Consulting Contract:** Contract for consulting services to be provided to the company by the executive after retirement. These contracts generally are provided to executives to enable them to complete projects that will extend past the executive's retirement date, or to give the company continued access to the experience of a respected executive.

**Post Retirement Dental:** Dental insurance coverage provided to the executive after he or she has retired from the company. The cost of post retirement dental coverage may be more expensive than pre-retirement plans due to the increasing use of medical services that generally occurs as people age.

**Post Retirement Life Insurance:** Personal life insurance coverage provided to executive after retirement.

**Post Retirement Medical Plan:** Medical coverage provided to retired executives. The cost of post retirement medical coverage may be more expensive than that of pre-retirement plans due to the increasing use of medical services that generally occurs as people age.

**Prescription:** Prescription insurance coverage provided to an individual after retirement. The cost of post retirement prescription coverage may be more expensive than that of pre-retirement plans due to the increasing use of medical services that generally occurs as people age.

**Privately-Held Corporation:** A company is a privately-held company if none of its equity securities is registered under the Securities Exchange Act of 1934.

**Professional Association Fees:** Company covers costs associated with executive's membership in professional associations. This normally includes all fees, dues, and related expenses. In certain fields, an individual must maintain a professional association membership to maintain a professional accreditation.

**Profit Sharing:** Plan in which employer agrees to make discretionary contributions (usually out of profits). The participant's retirement benefits are based on the amount in the individual account at retirement. A qualified capital accumulation plan in which an employer makes discretionary contributions to an employee's individual account, usually based on company profitability. A significant number of companies either require or allow employees to make additional contributions.

**Publicly-Traded Corporation:** A company is a publicly-traded company if it has a class of equity securities that is registered under the Securities Exchange Act of 1934 and, as a result, is subject to that Act's ongoing disclosure and reporting requirements.

**Qualified Capital Accumulation Plans:** A pension plan that meets the requirements of IRC (generally Section 401(a)). Qualified plans are eligible for special tax considerations. Employers are permitted to deduct contributions to the plan even though the benefits provided are deferred to a later date.

**Rabbi Trust:** One of several possible vehicles for funding a SERP. A rabbi trust is a fund used to accumulate deferred compensation. Contributions to the fund are tax-free until funds in trust are paid out, the employer gives up the right to recall the funds, or general creditors are given access to the funds.

**Retirement Planning:** Company pays for assisting the executive to plan for retirement. This normally entails integrating company provided retirement programs with other savings vehicles that the executive has accumulated from other sources. This service may be rendered by retirement planners selected either by the company or by the individual.

**Right to Purchase Company Car:** Right to purchase a company provided vehicle at the expiration of the auto lease or at the termination of the executive's employment.

**Salary Continuation Plan:** Program to continue an individual's base salary in the event the person is unable to work due to illness or injury. Salary continuation plans normally phase out after a certain period of time has elapsed and are replaced by long term disability and early retirement programs.

**S Corporation:** A corporation that meets the requirements of Section 1361 and makes a Section 1362(a) election and, as a result, is taxed as though the shareholders are carrying on their activities as partners. That is, the corporation pays no tax and the shareholders are taxed directly on the company's earnings.

**Secular Trust:** Fund used to accumulate deferred compensation. Contributions are taxable to the recipient as they are paid into the fund. The accumulated funds are paid to the recipient upon retirement.

**Severance Pay:** Predetermined plan that pays benefits (usually proportionate to length of employment) to employees undergoing a voluntary or involuntary separation from service. Executive severance plans can be negotiated individually or established by company policy. These severance arrangements are usually more generous and comprehensive than those available to the general employee population.

**Simplified Employee Pension (SEP):** Retirement program that takes the form of individual retirement accounts for all eligible employees. Contributions and eligibility are both subject to special rules.

**Split Dollar Insurance:** A type of life insurance plan that gives both the employer and the employee an interest in a cash-value life insurance policy on the employee's life. The plan may be owned by either the employer or the employee, as follows: if the employer owns the policy, the policy is endorsed to show the employee's beneficial interest (endorsement method); or, the employee owns the policy and makes a collateral assignment to the employer to evidence the employer's beneficial interest. The employee receives taxable income equal to the value of death benefit coverage paid for by the employer.

**Sports/Theater Tickets:** For the entertainment of company clients, companies may maintain season tickets or subscriptions to theatrical or sporting events. As a season ticket holder, the company need not scrounge for tickets to sell-out performances.

**Supplemental Disability Program:** Disability insurance provides income protection for accidents or illnesses that are not occupational in nature. Additional coverage of this kind may be offered to an executive to augment the standard disability program that covers the general employee population.

**Supplemental Executive Retirement Plan (SERP):** Pension plan (also known as a top-hat plan) that supplements the pension plan by giving credit for years of service or guaranteeing a specific benefit level after a minimum period of service. It is often used to augment a pension benefit, particularly in the case of an executive who joins a company at a senior level and will not have sufficient time to generate an adequate retirement benefit in the normal pension plan.

**Supplemental Long Term Disability Insurance:** Supplements to the long term disability programs offered to the general employee population include removing caps; greatly increasing benefit maximums; and increasing the period of time during which the executive is eligible to receive benefits.

**Tax Advice and Tax Return Preparation:** Executive is provided with personal tax counseling and advice, paid for by the company. This service may be rendered by a tax practitioner retained by the company or one chosen by the executive.

**Total Compensation:** Total compensation is comprised of an individual's base salary, annual incentives, long-term incentives, benefits, and executive perquisites.

**Travel Accident Insurance:** Life insurance that covers an individual while traveling on company business. This is coverage in addition to any other insurance programs the company provides.

**Unreasonable Compensation:** Unreasonable compensation is that portion of total compensation paid to an executive that exceeds what a similarly situated executive would be paid. The executive must include the unreasonable portion in his or her gross income. The company loses the compensation deduction for that portion of compensation that is deemed unreasonable.

**Use of Company Facilities on Vacation:** Executive has use of company owned facilities while on vacation. This is normally provided at low or no cost to the executive.

**Vision:** Vision insurance coverage provided to the executive after the individual has retired from the company. The cost of post retirement vision coverage may be more expensive than that of pre-retirement plans due to the increasing use of medical services that generally occurs as people age.

**Welfare Benefit Fund:** A fund created by an employer to pay welfare benefits to employees or to their beneficiaries pursuant to an employee benefit plan.

**Will Preparation:** Company pays for the drafting of an executive's personal will. This assistance may be rendered by an in-house attorney, one retained by the company, or one chosen by the executive.

# Index

*[References in the index are to question numbers.]*

## A

**Accounting Treatment**
Annual incentive plan, Q4:4
Capital accumulation plan, Q5:6,
Q5:13, Q5:14
Convertible debenture, Q6:57
Discounted stock option plan, Q6:26
Executive expenses, Q10:7, Q10:8
Executive perquisites, Q10:3
Incentive stock option plan, Q6:9
Nonstatutory option plan, Q6:17
Option reload plan, Q6:38
Performance unit plan, Q7:35
Phantom stock option, Q7:17
Premium stock option, Q6:33
Pyramiding, Q5:42
Restricted stock grant, Q7:26
Stock appreciation right, Q7:6
Stock swap, Q5:42
Tandem phantom stock/stock option plan, Q8:6
Tandem restricted stock/stock option plan, Q8:12
Tandem stock appreciation rights/stock option plan, Q8:19
**Alternate Investment**
Threshold levels, Q4:8
**Alternative Minimum Tax**
Rates, Q1:30, Q6:8

**Amendments**
To long-term incentive plan, Q5:45
**Annual Incentive Plan**
Accounting treatment of, Q4:4
Appropriateness of, Q1:13
Basic plan designs for, Q4:8
Definition, Q4:1
Feasibility of, Q1:14
Key issues in the design of, Q4:7
Performance standards for, Q4:26
Prevalence of, Q4:2
Rationale for, Q4:5
Tax impact of, Q4:3
Typical payment method, Q4:6
**Annual Plans**
vs. long-term, Q1:16
*See also* Annual Incentive Plan
**Appreciation Plan**
Definition, Q7:1
Examples of, Q7:2
**Automobiles**
Executive perquisite, Q10:9

## B

**Base Salary**
Definition, Q1:1
How determined, Q3:1, Q3:2
Market pricing, Q3:7

*[References in the index are to question numbers.]*

*[References in the index are to question numbers.]*

*[References in the index are to question numbers.]*

*[References in the index are to question numbers.]*

*[References in the index are to question numbers.]*

## Index

*[References in the index are to question numbers.]*

*[References in the index are to question numbers.]*

*[References in the index are to question numbers.]*

*[References in the index are to question numbers.]*

*[References in the index are to question numbers.]*

*[References in the index are to question numbers.]*

## Index